Published by Pedigree in association with **Yours**
Pedigree Books Limited, Beech House, Walnut Gardens, Exeter, Devon EX4 4DH
books@pedigreegroup.co.uk / www.pedigreebooks.com
**Yours** – the read of your life every fortnight!
Look out for it in your local newsagent.
**Yours**, Bauer London Lifestyle, Media House, Peterborough Business Park, Peterborough PE2 6EA.
Tel: 01733 468000

Compiled and edited by Sharon Reid
Designed by David Reid
Sub-edited by Christine Curtis
Additional writing by Marion Clarke, Rebecca Speechley, Michelle O'Neil, Sheena Correa, Gemma Toms
and gardening expert Gareth Salter
With grateful thanks to Garden Answers for the plant pictures

**Special thanks once again to the readers who have contributed so wonderfully to this Year Book
by sending in their memories, precious photographs, stories and tips**

◆ Please check with your GP if you're unsure about taking up any of our health tips,
especially if you are on medication.

◆ All telephone numbers, website details and dates correct at time of going to press

**W**elcome to A Year with **Yours** 2010. As usual it has been a joy to put together because essentially it's written for us by you, the readers of **Yours** magazine.

I always say that the best job as editor is reading the hundreds of letters and emails we receive each week. I love sharing your stories, hearing your funny anecdotes, understanding your concerns and looking at your photos. The only shame is that we can't print them all.

For A Year with **Yours** 2010 we've been able to include lots of **Yours** favourites – the hilarious Senior Moments and Small Talk – as well as a look back at how we dressed in Fashion We Wore. We've also managed to pack in delicious recipes, Plant Profiles, Health Tips and a whole host of fascinating facts. Along with short stories, quizzes and poems there really is enough to keep you reading throughout the year.

Happy reading – and all the best for 2010

Valery McConnell
Editor, **Yours**

# January 2010

Friday
## 1
New Year's Day

Saturday
## 2

Sunday
## 3

Monday
## 4
Bank Holiday (Scotland)

Tuesday
## 5

Wednesday
## 6
Epiphany

Thursday
## 7

Friday
## 8

Saturday
## 9

Sunday
## 10

Monday
## 11

Tuesday
## 12

Wednesday
## 13

Thursday
## 14

Friday
## 15

Saturday
## 16

Sunday
## 17

Monday
## 18

Tuesday
## 19

Wednesday
## 20

Thursday
## 21

Friday
## 22

| | |
|---|---|
| **Saturday** 23 | **Thursday** 28 |
| **Sunday** 24 | **Friday** 29 |
| **Monday** 25 — Burns' Night | **Saturday** 30 |
| **Tuesday** 26 | **Sunday** 31 |
| **Wednesday** 27 — Holocaust Memorial Day | |

## Poetry corner

# Diet diary

Have you ever stopped to think,
Of all the food we eat?
There's bacon, eggs, cheese and bread,
Biscuits, cake and meat.

Don't forget the ham and tongue,
The jelly and the rice,
The cherry pie and apple tart,
And carrot's that you dice.

Or how about a big steamed pud,
A bowl of prunes and custard?
A big pork chop with lots of chips,
And a nice pork pie with mustard?

So if you eat too many of these,
You'll surely feel a frump,
You'll find your clothes are rather tight,
And you'll end up round and plump!

**Angela Hickey, Middlesex**

# Village life

Ann (centre) wearing her new dress at Abram's annual Walking Day

I was brought up in a small mining village called Abram, just south of Wigan during the Fifties. We lived in a close-knit community where everyone knew everyone else. In a stretch less than two miles there were around 20 shops including a grocer, butcher, fish and chip shop, Post Office, hardware shop and drapers – everything you might need. The village had its own primary school, a lovely park, two pubs and three churches.

My own family life hinged around the Methodist Chapel, which was the centre of our social scene. The highlight of the year was the annual Walking Day. Banners would be carefully unfolded, little girls in new dresses carried bouquets, little boys wore silk trousers and adults wore their Sunday best. We all paraded through our village to the sounds of a brass band. Afterwards we had tea in the chapel and we then changed our clothes ready for games in the local farmer's field. What fun we had.

During the rest of the year we had several social evenings – potato pie suppers, talent evenings and our own concert party providing entertainment. A packed chapel was common and it wasn't unknown for chairs to be brought from the houses across the road. How different the area is now with only eight or nine shops remaining and just one church. Many of the green areas are housing estates and it seems very few people know each other.

**Ann Armstrong, Milton Keynes**

## Plant profile

### Clematis Cirrhosa Balearica

**Height: 3m**
**Spread: 1.8m**
**Conditions: Prefers well-drained soil in a sunny, sheltered position.**
An evergreen species, this charming climber flowers when little else is happening in the garden. Its pretty leaves turn an attractive shade of bronze in winter while its creamy-white blooms, which are speckled with maroon, produce a fresh citrus fragrance. It's hardier than others of its type and less vigorous, so grows well in a large container. Widely available from garden centres.

## Health tip
### One step at a time
Aim to change just one thing this New Year and you're more likely to stick to your health resolution. Choose whichever goal is most important to your health – quitting smoking, losing weight, eating healthier or getting fit.

## Senior moment

After returning home, I went to unlock the front door and wondered why it wouldn't open. I was pressing the remote button on my car key fob.

**Mrs Hawkins, Middlesex**

# Fast fact

During the 14th and 19th centuries it was a period of severe cold weather that became known as the Little Ice Age. The River Thames would often freeze over and Frost Fairs were held on the ice. Booths were set up and horse and coach races, football and bear-baiting would all take place.

# Small talk

While taking my four-year-old grandson George for a walk, a farmer had ploughed his fields and put goodness knows what on them. "Phew, what a smell," I said. As quick as a flash George said: "It's not me Gran." After much laughter I said: "It's not Gran either!"

**Mrs P Lawrence, Leicestershire**

# Fashion we wore

Here's a photo of me and my late mother-in-law (right) on our way to a wedding in 1963. My 'duster' coat was pale blue and under that I wore a white dress with a pattern in two shades of blue. My mother-in-law's suit was made of maroon velvet. She had already worn it to her own wedding the previous year. Much to our surprise we had both bought the exact same hat from the same shop. With our matching white shoes and handbags I think we looked quite a picture.

**Beryl Green, Manchester**

# Recipe of the week

## Green bean and prawn salad
Serves 4

For the dressing:
- Juice of 2 limes
- 1 tbsp fish sauce
- 1 medium red chilli, deseeded and finely sliced
- 1 tsp fresh ginger, finely grated
- 1 tsp caster sugar

For the salad:
- 250 g (10 oz) thin rice noodles (rice vermicelli)
- 1 tbsp toasted sesame oil
- 200 g (8 oz) green beans
- 200 g (8 oz) cooked, peeled prawns
- 1 bunch spring onions, finely sliced
- A large handful fresh coriander leaves, roughly chopped
- 2 tbsp salted peanuts, lightly crushed with a rolling pin

1. Mix all the dressing ingredients together in a small bowl and whisk. Set aside.
2. Place the rice noodles in a large heatproof bowl. Pour over enough boiling water to cover. Seal with a lid of cling-film and leave to soak for about 4 minutes, or until tender but still with a little bite. Drain and rinse with cold water to cool. Place in a large serving bowl and drizzle with sesame oil to prevent the noodles sticking together.
3. Cook the green beans in salted boiling water for 3-4 minutes, or until just tender. Drain and rinse under cold water. Slice each bean into 2-3 cm (1-2 in) pieces and add to the noodles.
4. Add the cooked prawns, sliced spring onions and chopped coriander to the noodles.
5. Pour over the dressing, toss well and serve immediately, scattered with the crushed peanuts.

Recipe: British Beans and Peas, www.tastesofsummer.co.uk

# My dad

I have a vivid memory of the first time I met my dad. When I was born the war was still going on but my dad hadn't been called up because the army only took men who were 100 per cent fit. You see Dad had some sort of injury when he was a small boy that resulted in his eye having to be removed.

However, when I was still a baby the powers that be got pretty desperate and they called up any adult male who could walk and hold a gun.

So, like many children born during the war, I didn't know my dad for the first few years of my life. The first time that I remember seeing him I must have been about three years old. My mum had gone to the shop across the road, leaving me and my older sister, Pat, in the house on our own. Suddenly this

Margaret's mum and dad

big tall stranger, wearing a funny uniform, a patch over one eye, came through the front door shouting, "Alice, it's me!"

I took one look at this one eyed monster and ran and hid behind the chair. I remember him bending down and picking up Pat and then trying to coax me out from behind the chair. One of the neighbours had obviously told Mum that Dad was back because she came rushing in. I ran to her screaming and she tried to calm me down saying, "Don't be silly, it's only your Dad!" But it didn't help. I refused to even look at him. Even when I was much older I still didn't like looking at his empty eye socket.

**Margaret Palmer, Peterborough**

## Plant profile

### Lonicera Purpusii 'Winter Beauty'

**Height: 1.9m**
**Spread: 3m**
**Conditions: Thrives in all but waterlogged soils and flowers best in full sun. Looks great trained against a south-facing wall.**
A member of the honeysuckle family, this variety produces sweetly fragrant, cream flowers in late winter and early spring. It makes an attractive shrub and should be positioned near a pathway so you can enjoy its scent. Widely available from garden centres.

## Health tip
### Be realistic

Set small achievable goals such as losing a pound a week or commit to walking twice round the block everyday. Setting out to lose two stones by the summer or planning to run a marathon in June will just set you up for failure. Small and simple is the secret to success.

## Senior moment

While out shopping in a well-known department store, I picked up a bright pink sweater. The lady opposite did the same so I smiled broadly and said, "Same good taste." The lady smiled back – it was me reflected in a large mirror! **C Styles, Staffs**

## Fast fact

The longest railway station name in the world is held by a Welsh town called Llanfairpwllgwyngyllgogerychwyrndrobwlllllantysiliogogogoch. With an amazing 58 letters in English it means; Saint Mary's Church in the hollow of white hazel near a rapid whirlpool and the Church of Saint Tysilio near the red cave.

## Small talk

Recently retired, I took my seven-year-old granddaughter to her gym lesson. We were a bit behind schedule so after parking the car, I jumped out and suggested we run in quickly. "Retired ladies don't run – Oh! Wait for me Grandma," she called. Guess who reached the door first!

**Vera Clay, Bristol**

## Fashion we wore

This is a photo of me, taken when I was 17 years old. I lived in the East End of London during the war with my parents and sister. This coat was so expensive that when I had finished with it, it was dyed and used as a rug for the fireplace! I took a lot of care with the accessories – notice the spotted gloves, elegant umbrella and the hat with a veil. I wish I had kept those shoes, although I couldn't walk in them now!

**Irene Joel, Brentwood, Essex**

## Recipe of the week

### Carrot, grapefruit and ginger super-juice
**Serves 2**

◆ 250 g (10 oz) Chantenay carrots
◆ 2 medium white grapefruit, peeled and cut into segments
◆ 15 g (¹/₂ oz) fresh ginger, unpeeled and left whole

1. Using a juicer, gradually feed the carrots, grapefruit and ginger into the machine.
2. When the juice has a thick consistency, turn off the juicer.
3. Using a spoon, mix well and pour into two glasses, over ice if desired.
4. Serve immediately

Recipe: Chantenay Carrots, www.chantenay.co.uk

## Go for it

Three years ago I was feeling drained by the effects of the menopause, so as a New Year's gift to myself I bought a copy of Paul McKenna's self-help book on confidence. According to the book when you're confident you take things on before you feel ready, in the knowledge that adrenalin will kick in.

I took this theory on board two years ago on a tour of New Zealand, when our Tour Manager Kevin told us one day that the weather was perfect for flying over Mount Cook. As a passenger I'd always flown in large aircraft and this tiny plane was a different challenge altogether. The old me would have bottled out, but this time I stunned my husband (and myself) by exclaiming that I'd like to go too! As soon as I'd uttered those words, unbelievably, fear

Margaret, chuffed after completing her flight

went out of the window. Paul McKenna was right – my adrenalin did kick in. I felt totally exhilarated and flying over the beautiful snow-capped Mount Cook was the most exciting hour I've ever spent. Somewhere in the back of my mind I was still aware that if we crashed there was an awful lot of snow under us. But the feeling of being so tantalizingly close to that sort of danger gave me such a buzz. Now my motto is don't wait until you feel ready to take on a challenge – just go for it.

**Margaret Turner, Warrington**

## Plant profile

### Sarcococca Confusa

**Height: 1.5m**
**Spread: 1.8m**
**Conditions: Loves a shady position in light, well-drained soil. Plant near a sheltered seating area to enjoy its sweet scent on a warm winter's day.**

Appearances are deceptive. Yes, this evergreen may look rather plain, but it has hidden depths. In late winter it produces small white flowers that are so richly scented they'll draw you back again and again and again, making gardening in winter a really enjoyable experience. Widely available from garden centres.

## Health tip

### It's never too late

If you haven't started getting healthy yet – it's not too late. In fact it's never too late according to US scientists. Adopting even the smallest healthy habit such as eating your five-a-day could add years to your life.

## Senior moment

We were on holiday where there were only hard paper toilet rolls. So when my husband went to the shops the next morning, I asked him to bring back half a dozen soft toilet rolls. Unfortunately, he didn't hear me properly and came back with half a dozen bread rolls!

**Marion Ward, Colchester**

## Fast fact

A A Milne, the creator of Winnie The Pooh, was born on 18 January, 1882. His famous storybook character was originally named Edward but was soon renamed after a Canadian Bear in London Zoo called Winnie and a swan called Pooh that lived near the family's home.

## Small talk

My granddaughter Lauren was given some glow-in-the-dark pyjamas by her aunty for her birthday. The following morning her mother asked, "Well, did they glow in the dark?" She replied, "How would I know? I was asleep."

**Lilian Smith, Preston**

## Fashion we wore

Here's a picture of me taken in Blackpool. I'm standing beside a borrowed car – we couldn't afford one of our own. The imitation fur coat was a gift from my future husband for Christmas 1959 – in fact it was an engagement present too. The ring followed at a later date on my 21st birthday in 1960. Our wedding was two years later and we have been happily married since.

**Janette McManus, Trowell, Notts**

# Recipe of the week

## Pea, smoked salmon and dill tart
### Serves 4

- 1 pack ready-rolled puff pastry
- 250 g (10 oz) Mascarpone cheese
- 2 tbsp fresh dill, finely chopped plus a tsp for decoration
- Juice of 1/2 a lemon
- 200 g (8 oz) pack of smoked salmon trimmings
- 100 g (4 oz) frozen peas, boiled
- Salt and freshly ground pepper

1. Preheat the oven to 200°C/400°F/Gas Mark 6
2. Unroll the puff pastry and cut down the length into 2 pieces. Lightly score a line 1 cm (½ in) round the edge of each piece.
3. In a mixing bowl, blend the Mascarpone with the dill and lemon juice and season well.
4. Using a blunt knife, spread evenly over the pastry, taking care to keep the mixture within the scored edges.
5. Cut the smoked salmon into thin ribbons and arrange with the peas over the top of the Mascarpone mix, pushing them lightly into cheese. It doesn't need to look too regimented, more of an artful scattering.
6. Bake both cases for 15-20 minutes, or until the pastry is crisp and golden.
7. Sprinkle with the extra dill and cut each pastry slice in half. Serve with a salad with a mix of peppery leaves like rocket or watercress.

Recipe: British Beans and Peas, www.tastesofsummer.co.uk

# My Daisy May

Sylvia's treasured Daisy May

**T**his beautiful doll found in a small antique shop brought back fond memories of my beloved Daisy May. Growing up I shared a bedroom with my elder sister who was 17 years older than me. At the bottom of my sister's bed sat a large doll's pram and inside was a beautiful doll called Daisy May. Grandma had given it to my aunt before it was handed down to my sister in the 1930s. The pram was always covered with a large dustsheet keeping the doll and pram clean.

My sister didn't like me playing with the doll, but while she was at work I often used to undress her and try her in different outfits. Unfortunately, being small I couldn't always remember which of her lovely dresses I'd taken off and there were many times I was told off for not correctly dressing her.

I was five when my sister told me she was getting married and that I was going to be a bridesmaid. The wedding dress, bridesmaids dresses and my brother's suit were all made by my Aunts who were dressmakers. There were many fittings for the dress – and many tantrums. One day my sister told me she had something for me. The cover was removed from the pram and she gently placed the doll in my arms making me promise to take good care of her. How this antique shop doll, so like my Daisy May, revived many happy childhood memories.

**Sylvia Smallwood, Cheshire**

## Plant profile

### Cyclamen Coum

**Height: 8cm**
**Spread: 15cm**
**Conditions: Thrives in most soils but prefers a well-drained situation in the shade of deciduous trees.**
Producing dainty blooms between late winter and early spring, this pretty plant looks great in an alpine bed or in the leafy undergrowth of a woodland garden. The green leaves, which are mottled silver, are a perfect backdrop for the purple, pink or white flowers. Mulch annually to prevent the tubers from drying out. Available online from www.dejager.co.uk, it has an Award of Garden Merit from the RHS.

## Health tip
### Stretch!

Don't underestimate the power of a good stretch – it helps to keep your joints supple and strong and could help to ease aches and pains. For top notch stretching join a Hatha Yoga class – contact the British Wheel of Yoga www.bwy.org.uk to find out more.

## Senior moment

I bought my first mobile phone, I only had it a week and returned it informing the salesman that it was hopeless and I couldn't even get a line. He replied, "You won't, mobiles don't have lines." What a fool I felt! **Jennifer Parker, Worcs**

## Fast fact

Elephants are one of the few mammals that continue to grow throughout their lifetimes and can reach up to 13ft in height at their shoulders. They can live up to 70 years and they have the largest brains found in the animal kingdom.

## Small talk

I was making lunch and asked my granddaughter, Anna, aged five to ask her Mum what colour of milk she wanted, red, green or blue. She looked at me with a puzzled expression and said, "Mummy always buys white milk."

**Mrs S Hurst, Bolton**

## Fashion we wore

**T**his snap of me and my mother, Lilly, was taken by my husband, Cliff. We were dressed up for the wedding of Ann and Doug Tyson in September 1954. My mother-in-law made my dress and bag for me out of pale pink 'grow-grain' under a layer of black lace. I remember she bought the material in Roman Road Market, Bow for 7s. Cliff's mum was 65 at the time – not bad dressmaking skills for a lady of that age!

**Kathleen Tanner, Ramsgate**

## Recipe of the week

PIC: STEVE BAXTER

### Melt-in-the-middle caramel berry bars

**Makes 12**

- ◆ 300 g (12 oz) eating apples, peeled, cored and diced
- ◆ 397 g (16 oz) can Carnation Caramel
- ◆ 200 g (8 oz) whole porridge oats
- ◆ 2tsp cinnamon, optional

For the crumbly topping:
- ◆ 50 g (2 oz) whole porridge oats
- ◆ 15 g (1 oz) butter, finely cubed
- ◆ 50 g (2 oz) flaked almonds, toasted
- ◆ 300 g (12 oz) fresh or frozen forest fruits

1. Preheat the oven to 180°C/350°F/Gas Mark 4. Line an 18 x 28cm (7 x 11 in) baking tin.
2. In a saucepan, add the apple with 6 tablespoons of water, cover and lightly simmer for 5-6 minutes, or until soft. Drain the excess water and purée in a blender or mash with a potato masher.
3. Using a large mixing bowl, mix the oats and cinnamon before adding the cooked apple and two-thirds of the caramel. Mix well.
4. Spread two-thirds of the oat mixture onto the base of the baking tin and push into the corners with the back of a wooden spoon to form a smooth layer.
5. Sprinkle the berries on top of the base. Beat the remaining caramel in the can and drizzle over the berries.
6. For the topping, add the remaining oats to the mixture in the bowl and stir. Add the butter and almonds and use your fingers to mix well.
7. Dot over the berries and gently press down to combine all the layers. Bake for 25-30 minutes, or until golden brown. Leave to cool completely before cutting into squares. Enjoy with a blob of clotted cream.

Recipe: Nestle Carnation, www.carnation.co.uk

# I remember big hair

BY: MARION CLARKE

It started in the 1970s with Charlie's Angels star, Farrah Fawcett, who was the undisputed trendsetter for big hair. Her abundant wavy tresses were the envy of every woman. To get the same look, we had to endure sleepless nights with our own mousy locks wrapped round giant, prickly curlers – each one anchored with a cruel, scalp piercing pin. Failing that, we had to set the alarm to get up early and put in our Carmen heated rollers for 15 minutes before we faced the world.

## Looking back... it's hard not to giggle

Then along came the 1980s – and Dynasty, the soap opera that made padded shoulders and big hair fashionable for a decade. This was a look that was all about women and power. Joan Collins, playing super bitch Alexis Carrington, led the way with shoulders like a guardsman and a bouffant backcombed style that was slavishly copied by millions. Sales of hairspray soared as we struggled to keep those elaborate topknots in place through the day.

Looking back at old photos, it's hard not to giggle. We looked a lot like Danny La Rue in drag but we thought we were glamorous!

Poor Pamela Sue Martin, who played Fallon in Dynasty, has since confessed that her own locks were thinning fast and the producers made her wear a wig to achieve the big hair demanded

The late Farrah Fawcett set the trend with her big wavy locks we all envied.

PIC: REX FEATURES

for the role.

Another big hair look that was popular at the time was the Afro, inspired by the Black Power movement. This was fine for women like Caribbean singer Joan Armatrading who had a genuine Afro but for white women there was only one

solution – the frizzy perm!

Dutifully, we all trooped off to the salon to have our dead straight bobs tortured into a crinkly tangle that was impossible to get a brush through. Instead we became expert at flicking it up and out with wide-toothed wooden combs to make it look as big as possible.

# Quiz of the month

All these events took place in the month of January over the past 60 years, but can you arrange them in the order that they happened?

PIC: REX FEATURES

**I** Sir Winston Churchill has died at the age of 90, with his wife Lady Clementine Churchill and other members of the family at his bedside.

**J** Teenager Derek Bentley hanged for murder at Wandsworth Prison in London for his part in the murder of PC Sidney Miles.

**K** The American space shuttle, Challenger, has exploded killing all seven astronauts on board, including the first teacher in space.

**L** The first jumbo jet, carrying fare-paying passengers, arrives at Heathrow airport.

**M** The Gulf War Allies have sent hundreds of planes on bombing raids into Iraq, at the start of Operation Desert Storm.

**N** The music publisher EMI has ended its contract with the Sex Pistols punk rock group because of their notorious behaviour in public.

**O** The number of people out of work and claiming benefit has risen above one million for the first time since the 1930s.

**P** The United Kingdom has become a fully-fledged member of the European Economic Community.

News stories taken from http://news.bbc.co.uk/onthisday/

**A** Dame Agatha Christie, has died, leaving rumours of a multi-million pound fortune and a final book waiting to be published.

**B** Harold Macmillan has accepted the Queen's invitation to become Prime Minister following the sudden resignation of Sir Anthony Eden.

**C** Hollywood star Marilyn Monroe has divorced her husband, playwright Arthur Miller, after less than five years of marriage.

**D** Indira Gandhi, only daughter of India's first Prime Minister Jawaharlal Nehru, is to become the country's next leader.

**E** It's now compulsory for drivers and front seat passengers to wear seatbelts under a new law which, it is hoped, will save 1,000 lives a year.

**F** People have been switching on their televisions a little earlier than usual to catch Britain's first breakfast news programme, presented by Frank Bough and Selina Scott.

**G** Serial killer Fred West, the Gloucestershire builder charged with 12 murders, has been found dead in his prison cell.

**H** Sir Edmund Hillary reaches the South Pole – the first overland explorer to do so since Captain Robert F Scott's expedition in 1912.

Answer: J) 1953, B) 1957, H) 1958, C) 1961, I) 1965, D) 1966, L) 1970, O) 1972, P) 1973, A) 1976, N) 1976, F) 1977, E) 1982, K) 1983, M) 1986, N) 1991, G) 1995

# In a bit of a spin

BY: JANICE SADLER

## Charlie has more than the washday blues…

Charlie hated going to the launderette. The first problem was the door. It always stuck on a wonky tile so it only opened six inches, nowhere near wide enough for him to get through carrying that stupid yellow laundry basket.

"That door sticks," said a voice from within. "Time somebody mended it."

Charlie felt the clammy heat engulf him as he stood with one foot jammed against the doorframe and the basket pressed into his stomach.

Inside, lined up like children playing musical chairs, Charlie could see several ladies. One of them got up wearily and walked over to the door which she yanked open with a deft flick of her wrist.

"Don't hang about on the step," she said. "You're letting the cold in."

## Lined up like children playing musical chairs

"Sorry," mumbled Charlie, thinking, 'Gaining a degree in French? No problem. Teaching a class of 30 teenagers? Easy. Opening the launderette door? Impossible!'.

He began to load his dirty underwear into a machine. Suddenly he felt a prod in his back.

"That's a dryer," a voice told him. "The washers are over there."

Under close scrutiny, he pulled everything out and trailed it across to a washing machine. The floor was strewn with shirts, socks and underpants.

Charlie cursed the fact that he and Lizzie had never got round to buying a washing machine. He was to blame – she'd told him often enough she wanted one.

But somehow there always seemed to be something more exciting to do with their spare cash. Like buying an old van to travel around France, camping under the stars.

Charlie swallowed hard. If only he'd behaved like a proper husband. If only he'd bought her a washing machine…

A sign on the wall advised customers whose laundry weighed more than 22 pounds to use one of the big machines. Charlie glared at it. How was he supposed to know how much his laundry weighed? There were no scales available so he chose a machine at random.

"Excuse me," said a voice behind him.

Charlie swung round.

"I don't know if you've noticed but…"

"What?"

"You've put a red, er, garment in there."

Charlie stared at the lady, who said: "The colour will run. Then all your stuff will end up pink."

"Oh, right," said Charlie, feeling around inside the drum.

As he fumbled in his pocket for the right change, he could hear the ladies tut-tutting. Ignoring them, he reached into his basket for the washing powder. He'd forgotten to bring it! Charlie felt his audience exchanging pitying glances.

He set the temperature dial as hot as it would go in the hope that a good boil would make up for the lack of detergent. Someone tapped his shoulder.

"Do you want to sit down?" It was the lady who'd opened the door for him.

Unable to answer, Charlie made straight for the door. Seconds later, he was in his car and the tears began to flow…

By Monday, Charlie felt better. With the long, lonely weekend behind him, he could get back to work. Once in his classroom, maybe the days wouldn't seem so empty. But where was the pleasure in ending a day at work if he didn't have Lizzie to come home to?

The week passed and the yellow laundry basket filled up again. All too soon, Saturday morning came round.

Balancing the basket on his knee, Charlie leaned against the glass door. It flew open and he tumbled into the launderette, where the lady who'd come to his rescue before confronted him.

"I had a word with the manager," she explained, then pointed to the washing machines. On top of one of them sat a pair of scales.

"We've been pestering him for ages to get scales,"

PIC: KATE DAVIES

# "You made your wife the happiest woman in the world"

she added. "I mean, how's a person supposed to know what 22 pounds of washing looks like?"

Charlie's jaw dropped. "That's just what I thought!"

He piled his dirty washing onto the scales then loaded his greyish shirts and off-white handkerchiefs into a small machine. He closed the door and rummaged in his pocket for the right money.

He felt a tap on his shoulder.

"There's a change machine on that wall," said one of the ladies.

Charlie stared. "Has that always been there?"

"Yes, but it's usually empty."

Slotting the coins into the machine, Charlie relaxed. All he needed now was the powder. He reached into the yellow basket. It was empty!

"Would you like to use some of mine?" asked a voice at his side.

"Oh, I couldn't…"

"I always bring too much. Saves me having to carry it home." She trickled the right amount into the slot then set the temperature dial to Cool Cottons.

"Thank you," said Charlie.

"You're welcome," replied the lady. "My name's Mrs Jarvis but you can call me Kath."

"And I'm-"

"Charlie," said Kath.

Charlie was amazed. "How do you know my name?"

"Oh, I know a lot about you!" laughed Kath.

Charlie was intrigued. "Like what?"

"Like how you travelled around France in an old van."

Charlie's eyes grew wide.

"And you bought a tent and slept under the stars."

Then the lady whose name he hadn't known five minutes ago gently took his hand and said: "And how you made your wife the happiest woman in the world."

Charlie's voice was a whisper: "You knew Lizzie?"

"Of course, I knew Lizzie! Didn't she used to come in here every Saturday?"

Charlie nodded. "She did."

"She was a lovely girl," said Kath, wiping away a tear.

"Yes," agreed Charlie. "Yes, she was." And he felt, at last, a kind of peace.

# February 2010

Monday
1

Tuesday
2

Wednesday
3

Thursday
4

Friday
5

Saturday
6

Sunday
7

Monday
8

Tuesday
9

Wednesday
10

Thursday
11

Friday
12

Saturday
13

Sunday
14

**St Valentine's Day**

Monday
15

Tuesday
16

**Shrove Tuesday (Pancake Day)**

Wednesday
17

**Ash Wednesday**

Thursday
18

Friday
19

Saturday
20

Sunday
21

Monday
22

Tuesday

# 23

Wednesday

# 24

Thursday

# 25

Friday

# 26

Saturday

# 27

Sunday

# 28

## Poetry corner

# Dream date

I'm looking for a fella, 70 plus,
But please don't think I'm making a fuss.
For he has to be someone to share a joke,
I couldn't put up with a grumpy old bloke.

I like to go dancing so he has to be tall,
I don't want to look like a foxtrotting fool,
With me looking down on his bald head,
I'd much rather look up his nose instead.

I don't want a toyboy who looks like my son,
I just want someone to share some fun.
And I don't want a man with a one-track mind,
I just want someone who's loving and kind.

I'd like a companion to share my days,
As long as he hasn't any funny old ways.
I'd like to be spoilt for the rest of my life,
But not necessarily becoming his wife.
As this ideal man is yet to be seen,
I'll just sit here, and wish and dream!

**Irene Purslow, Birmingham**

# Saturday afternoons

**M**y Saturday afternoons when I was 15, in 1957, were spent in an upstairs flat directly above the only music shop in the small town of Whitley Bay, Northumberland. My friend Jan and I would lay with our eardrums pressed closely to the floral carpet listening to the pulsating music below. The Teddy Boys wearing coloured drapes and blue suede crêpe-soled shoes would be slouching nonchalantly against the counter. The girls wearing full skirts over petticoats starched stiff with sugar and water, would be huddled together smiling coquettishly at the boys through pale pink lips.

We listened to the throbbing rhythm of Elvis Presley singing Jailhouse Rock and longed to be down there. But Elvis was considered improper

Irene's forbidden utopia – Spanish City in Whitley Bay

among the so-called middle class parents of us sheltered grammar school girls. At 5pm the music would cease and the teenagers would pour out into the street below. Teds would strut their stuff down the street followed closely by giggling girls. We knew, with envy, that they were heading for the sea front and our forbidden utopia called the Spanish City. With its wonderful white dome and fairground rides including the helter-skelter, the big dipper, the dive-bomber and best of all the waltzers. Unknown to our parents we did go there and we tried hard to emulate the real thing, but of course we could only ever be pseudo teddy girls. Nevertheless, we hung around the jukebox trying to look blasé while swaying to the sounds of Bobby Darin, the Everly Brothers and Elvis.

**Irene Brown, Tyne and Wear**

## Plant profile

### Helleborus Niger

**Height: 50cm**
**Spread: 50cm**
**Conditions: Thrives in fertile, well-drained, soils, especially those that remain moist. Neutral or slightly alkaline soils and partial shade are preferred.**
Although this species is commonly called the Christmas rose, it tends to flower several weeks later in the year, usually between December and March. Its large, round, white flowers shine out against the leathery leaves. Widely available from garden centres, it has an Award of Garden Merit from the RHS.

## Health tip
### Check your salt

Spend a week logging how much salt you eat by reading food labels. High blood pressure is a major cause of stroke and eating less salt could help to keep yours lower say researchers. Aim for less than 6g a day.

## Senior moment

I was going to a funeral and had planned to wake up early. I looked at the clock and it was 6:10am, so I got up and had my shower and breakfast. Then went into the lounge to find it was actually 2:30am and I had read the hands of the clock the wrong way. At least I was in plenty of time for the funeral!

**Beryl Trevethick, Solihull**

## Fast fact

In 1960 American actress Joanne Woodward, who was also married to the late Paul Newman, was the first person ever to receive a star on the Hollywood Walk of Fame. There are now well over 2000 stars.

## Small talk

My three-year-old granddaughter, Gracie, dropped her biscuit on the kitchen floor. "Pick it up and throw it in the bin," I said to her. She answered: "Nana, you don't say throw it in the bin, you say chick it in the bin." I think she will be a true Yorkshire lass!

**Eileen Hicks, South Yorkshire**

## Fashion we wore

This picture was taken in 1962. I'm standing with my colleagues, Jean and Jackie, who I worked with at the School Psychological and Child Guidance Unit. We were on our way to another colleague's wedding. I'm on the left wearing a red suit, with blue bag and gloves. I was 17 years old at the time and left the job just before my next birthday, which I spent working in Butlins, Skegness as a shop assistant.

**Ann Carrier, Market Harborough**

# Recipe of the week

## Leek and bread pudding
**Serves 4**

◆ 3 tbsp Rapeseed Oil
◆ 400 g (16 oz) leeks, washed, trimmed and sliced into 1cm (½ in) pieces
◆ 6 thick slices wholemeal bread
◆ 100 g (4 oz) low-fat soft cheese
◆ 4 medium eggs, beaten
◆ 150 ml (6 fl oz) semi-skimmed milk

1. Preheat the oven to 180C/350°F/Gas Mark 4.
2. In a large frying pan, heat the oil before frying the leeks for 5 minutes, until softened.
3. Spread the bread with the cream cheese and cut each slice into quarters. Place half in the bottom of a heatproof dish, cheese side up. Scatter half the leeks over the top.
4. Mix the eggs, milk and season. Pour half over the leeks, and repeat with the remaining bread, then leeks before pouring over the remaining egg mixture. Bake for 25 minutes, or until golden brown and set.

Recipe: Rapeseed Oil, www.hgca.com

# My Dream

Two years ago I was in a bad place in my life. My father had been diagnosed with bladder and lung cancer and then suffered a stroke and my mother was also in poor health. As the only driver in the family I took them both to all of their appointments and was 'on call' if either of them needed me. I felt unhappy at work and I wasn't happy where I was living either. I often worked night shifts and when the menopause hit I found sleeping very difficult. Before long I was visiting the doctor suffering from stress, depression and high blood pressure. I felt like my life was out of control, but I was helpless. I had a dream of retiring early and moving to North Yorkshire, but it felt far out of reach. I couldn't afford to give up my job and I would never leave my dad. When his health

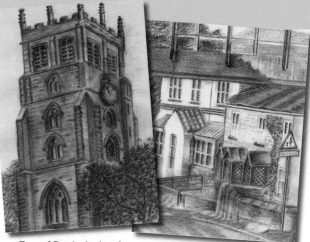

Two of Denise's sketches

deteriorated and he passed away I was devastated, but it was also a wake up call. I sold my house, moved in with my mother and applied for early retirement. I bought a small mobile home on a quiet, picturesque park in North Yorkshire. It's less than an hour's drive from my mother's house and is open all year so I spend most of my time there. I had to compromise on some parts of my dream, but all the important components are intact. Now I feel settled in this beautiful countryside I've resumed long-neglected hobbies of sketching, painting and writing.

**Denise Tuck, Tyne & Wear**

## Plant profile

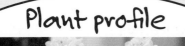

### Narcissus 'Paperwhite'

**Height:** 35cm
**Spread:** 15cm
**Conditions:** Thrives in moist, well-drained soil and full sun.

Producing around ten flowers per stem, this miniature daffodil looks amazing in early spring, its white blooms so highly-scented that they'll brighten any room. If you miss buying them as bulbs during the autumn (when you can plant them inside and bring them on to bloom at Christmas), look out for ready-planted containers during spring. Widely available from garden centres.

## Health tip
### Beat the blues

If February is getting you down, lift your mood by tucking into a plate of spaghetti bolognaise made with wholegrain pasta. Wholegrain foods help your brain to make the mood-boosting hormone serotonin.

## Senior moment

I was house-sitting for my grandson while a carpet was being fitted. The fitter took off his shirt and put his overalls on. I was ironing at the time and when he had done he couldn't find his shirt anywhere. We eventually realised I had ironed it and put it away with my grandson's shirts.

**Mrs A Stewart, Rotherham**

## Fast fact

Author Charles Dickens was born on 7 February, 1812 and published his first novel aged just 25. He is said to have always slept with his head facing towards the north and when he wrote he would always sit facing the north, too.

## Small talk

My granddaughter was with me visiting her granddad in hospital, who was suffering from a bad reaction to his medicine. He was wired up to all sorts of machines, and as he lay on his side the machine gave a loud beep. "Granddad's cooked," she announced.          **Gillian Muir, London**

## Fashion we wore

This photo was taken in 1949, when I was just 19 years old. My boyfriend at the time wanted a full-length photo of me taken in a studio. I had just recently bought the coat – a 'New Look' style in bright red. I also had on my first pair of black high-heeled suede shoes. I remember so clearly what I felt like getting ready – I wanted to look just right for him. He thought I looked really special and I felt like the Queen.
**Celia Wadsworth, Solihull**

## Recipe of the week

PIC: STEVE BAXTER

### Fudgy chocolate croissant pudding

Serves 4-6

- 4 chocolate croissants
- 100 g (4 oz) dark chocolate, roughly broken into pieces
- 300 ml (½ pt) milk
- 568 ml (20 fl oz) carton double cream
- Pinch of freshly grated nutmeg
- 4 large egg yolks
- 170g (7 oz) tube Carnation Condensed Milk
- Icing sugar, to dust

1. Lightly grease a 2¼ litre (4 pt) ovenproof dish.
2. Slice each croissant into three and arrange in the dish. Place the chocolate in a saucepan with the milk, cream and nutmeg and gently heat until the chocolate has melted.
3. In a large mixing bowl, whisk together the egg yolks and the condensed milk, then gradually beat in the hot chocolate cream.
4. Pour the mixture over the croissants, then gently press them down to help soak up the mixture. Leave to stand for 1 hour.
5. In the meantime, preheat the oven to 180°C/ 350° F/Gas Mark 4.
6. Place the dish into a deep roasting tin and fill the tin with enough boiling water to come two-thirds up the sides of the dish. Bake for 30–40 minutes, or until just set and a bit wobbly. Dust liberally with icing sugar and serve immediately.

Recipe: Nestlé Carnation, www.carnation.co.uk

# Self-sufficiency

In the late Seventies my husband and I decided we'd like to move to the country and reach a level of 'self sufficiency'. We soon found our perfect home – a cottage on the towpath of a canal with a rowing boat moored in front of it. We couldn't wait to gather our livestock and a friend in South Wales got us started with a white goat named Daisy and six white ducks. As we wanted to have our own milk supply, we took Daisy to a Billy goat and after months of us fussing excitedly she produced three little snowy white kids. Our menagerie was growing! Vicious Victor and Friendly Fred were two cockerels donated by another friend and they were joined by 24 rescued battery hens – with barely a feather between them.

In the summer holiday, we swapped houses for

Shirley and her snowy white kids

two weeks with some friends. By this time we were milking Daisy regularly. After we departed, foul language could apparently be heard coming from the goat hut. Every time a teacup full of milk was in the bucket Daisy would lift her leg and put her foot in it! We returned to find our baby ducks in a paddling pool on the lawn having their first swimming lesson and the guinea fowl had flown off never to be seen again. Apart from a good quantity of milk and a few eggs our self-sufficiency wasn't very profitable. But, we have some wonderful memories of our four years in the cottage by the canal.

**Shirley Carpenter, Somerset**

## Plant profile

### Galanthus 'Bertram Anderson'

**Height: 25cm**
**Spread: 8cm**
**Conditions: Snowdrops thrive in well-drained soil and dappled shade.**

If one plant heralds the end of winter more than any other, it's the snowdrop. Coping with the iciest weather, it flowers happily from late January onwards, looking best when allowed to naturalise in the grass beneath trees.
This variety has exceptionally large flowers and is available from specialist nurseries such as Cotswold Garden Flowers. Dry bulbs take a while to establish so transplant plants while 'in the green'.

## Health tip
### Make a commitment

Commit to doing 30 minutes of an activity that gets you hot and sweaty everyday. Canadian researchers say that regular exercise could help you to slow down the ageing process by up to 12 years!

## Senior moment

My wife phoned Tesco to confirm that the ink cartridges I needed for my printer were in stock at our local store. So I was mystified when I later went to the customer service desk to be told they didn't have any. I explained that my wife had just phoned Tesco and was told they were available. The young lady politely replied: "Perhaps you should try there then sir – this is Sainsbury's."

**Keith Maile, St Ives**

## Fast fact

A pair of doves will often mate for life. Superstition says that doves find their mate on St Valentine's Day, so if you're lucky enough to see a pair of doves on February 14 – you too may be lucky in love.

## Small talk

Bethany, my granddaughter, heard the windpipe mentioned on a vet programme on TV, and asked her mother if it was in the horse's bottom! **Mrs V Bray, Hants**

## Fashion we wore

**H**erc's a snap of me and two friends, taken at Seaton Carew in 1948. We've been friends since our school days. Hilda Parker is on the left, wearing a maroon dress and brown jacket. Irene is in the centre, wearing a grey and black jacket and black skirt. I'm on the right, wearing a blue jacket, brown skirt and a jumper that I'd knitted myself. We've all kept in touch – in fact Irene and I married brothers – and we meet up every week for lunch.

**Lillian Hogg, Hartlepool**

# Recipe of the week

## Indian–spiced broccoli and carrot salad

**Serves 4**

- ◆ 200g (8 oz) pack Tenderstem® broccoli
- ◆ 3 medium carrots
- ◆ 2 tbsp olive oil
- ◆ 2 tbsp mustard seeds
- ◆ 1 heaped tsp garam masala
- ◆ 1 heaped tsp ground cumin
- ◆ Juice of 1 lemon
- ◆ A large handful of coriander, roughly chopped

1. Shave 3 medium carrots lengthways into long strips using a vegetable peeler.
2. Steam or boil the Tenderstem® broccoli for 2 minutes, or until almost tender, then add the carrot strips for a further 1 minute. Drain and keep warm.
3. While the vegetables are cooking, take a small frying pan and add the olive oil. Heat before frying the mustard seeds until they start to pop.
4. Then add the garam masala and ground cumin. Give the pan a quick shake to mix then tip into a small clean bowl before the spices start to burn.
5. Add the lemon juice and season to taste.
6. Pour the dressing over the vegetables and toss gently to coat evenly. Sprinkle over the coriander and serve immediately with warm naan bread and thick natural yoghurt.

Recipe: Tenderstem® broccoli, www.tenderstem.co.uk

# Holidays in Margate

Dianne with her mum and sister Joan on holiday in Margate in 1946

In 1946, a year after the war ended, our parents took us for a holiday in Margate. We had no car so the prospect of travelling by train was so exciting that my sister, Joan, and I hardly slept the night before. The next morning, we could hardly contain our excitement when on reaching the platform the train came into view belching large clouds of steam and hissing noisily. On our arrival in Margate we found the boarding house, where we would be staying. Joan and I had our own room and there was a bathroom with hot and cold running water. At home we only had an outside toilet and no bathroom, just a tin bath.

The weather was fine, warm and sunny and we spent most of the days playing on the beach and swimming in the sea. In the evenings our parents would sometimes take us to an amusement park called Dreamland where we would be allowed to play on the various slot machines and sideshows. After the long, dark wartime years it was absolute heaven. The week passed all too quickly and we were heartbroken on the final night knowing that our holiday was over. The memories of that wonderful holiday have lasted for more than fifty years. As sisters, and also best friends, we have since shared many fantastic holidays both in England and abroad, but our Margate holiday has extra special memories for both of us. **Dianne Pitts, Middlesex**

## Plant profile

### Corylus Avellana 'Contorta'

**Height: 3m**
**Spread: 3.5m**
**Conditions: Hazels thrive in most soils and enjoy sun or partial shade.**

The corkscrew hazel, so called for its weirdly twisted stems, is at its best during early spring when fluffy yellow catkins hang decoratively from its branches. Although it eventually gets quite large, it grows slowly and can be pruned hard back. The bare stems look amazing against a clear blue sky during winter. Widely available from garden centres, it has an Award of Garden Merit from the RHS.

## Health tip
### Be positive

If you're optimistic and trusting you may well live longer than your cynical friends. Positive folk are 30 per cent less likely to die of heart disease according to scientists. Start giving everything a 'glass-half-full' spin.

## Senior moment

I'd prepared vegetables for my evening meal and was just putting them in the saucepan, when I realised that I had already been out with a friend to a local pub a few hours earlier and had eaten my dinner with her! **Mrs V A Piggott, Beds**

## Fast fact

Bookkeeper is the only word in the English language that has three continuing double-letter combinations (oo kk ee). Squirreled is the longest English word that has only one syllable.

## Small talk

We were out walking in the fields when our grandson, Edward, aged four, noticed a pile of horse manure. I told him that when I was young I used to collect it for my dad's rhubarb, and Mum made rhubarb pies. Edward walked in silence for a while, and then said: "I don't like rhubarb pie –it's made of horse poo!" **Ann Hooker, Derbyshire**

## Fashion we wore

This photograph was taken around 1946, in the grounds of Rhuddlan Castle. I'm third from the left in this line-up of the Rhuddlan Morris Dancers. It was hard work learning the dances and the weather in North Wales was often cold and unpredictable, especially for Easter parades. I remember Mum said that I had to choose between being in the Girl Guides or the dance troupe. I had been a Brownie and Girl Guide for as long as I could remember but when I started dancing Mum said we couldn't afford both. The dance troupe seemed so grown-up and exciting by comparison and as the picture shows I made my choice.

**Patricia Emery, Southampton**

# Recipe of the week

## Caramel flan
**Serves 6-8**

◆ 200 g (8 oz) caster sugar
◆ 600 ml (1 pt) milk
◆ Zest and juice of 1 lemon
◆ Zest of 1 orange
◆ 3 large Lion Quality eggs
◆ 3 large Lion Quality egg yolks
◆ 2 medium oranges, peeled and segmented for decoration

1. Preheat the oven to 150°C/300°F/Gas Mark 2.
2. In a medium saucepan, gently heat 175 g (7 oz) of the caster sugar, stirring occasionally until it dissolves. Gradually add the lemon juice and stir until the bubbling stops. Pour over the base of a 900 ml ($1^{1}/_{2}$ pt) round ovenproof dish.
3. Swirl the dish to coat the base and sides with the caramel and set aside.
4. Add the milk to the caramel saucepan with the lemon and orange zest and slowly bring to the boil.
5. Leave to cool, then strain into a large mixing bowl to discard the zest. Beat the eggs and remaining sugar together and beat into the milk. Pour into the caramel lined dish. Place in a roasting tin and pour boiling water to come halfway up the outside of the pudding dish.
6. Bake for 35-40 minutes, or until just set but still a little wobbly in the centre. Leave to cool before chilling for at least 4 hours.
7. To serve, turn the pudding onto a serving plate; cut into wedges and serve decorated with the orange segments.

Recipe: British Lion Eggs, www.eggrecipes.co.uk

# I remember coffee bars

## BY: MARION CLARKE

Formica-topped tables, pyrex cups and saucers, the hissing steam of the Gaggia coffee machine competing with the juke-box – coffee bars were the place to be if you were young in the Fifties and Sixties. The customers ranged from earnest young men in duffel coats sporting Ban the Bomb badges to office girls with bouffant back-combed hair giggling and chatting over endless cups of 'frothy coffee'.

The 'froth' was the result of a high pressure extraction feature on Gaggia's espresso machines that produced a thick layer of cream – christened a cappuccino because it was thought to be the same colour as the robes worn by Capuchin monks. Skinny lattes and Americanos were, as yet, unheard of variations.

Soho in London boasted the most, and arguably the best, coffee bars in the country. The first one, The Mokka in Frith Street, was opened by glamorous Italian film star Gina Lollabrigida in 1953. But the most famous

## 2i's was famous for putting on live music

Soho coffee bar was undoubtedly the 2i's in Old Compton Street. Owned by Paul Lincoln, an Australian wrestler, the 2i's was famous for putting on live music in the basement.

Tommy Steele and Cliff Richard played their early gigs at the 2i's coffee bar

PIC: REX FEATURES

Skiffle was popular at the time, especially with the students and beatniks who haunted the coffee bars, but rock 'n' roll was also beginning to be heard. Some of the stars who had their first gigs in the basement of the 2i's were Tommy Steele, Cliff Richard, Screaming Lord Sutch and Mickie Most.

Outside London, every town soon had its coffee bar, many of them part of the Kardomah chain, owned by Forte's. They all had suitably exotic names like El Kabala or the Cuba, distinguishing them from old fashioned tea rooms with cosy names like The Copper Kettle.

Tea rooms were for the respectable and the middle-aged while coffee bars were the venue for the young, bohemians, would-be intellectuals and poets. Although he later became famous for his fondness for stronger beverages, the Welsh poet Dylan Thomas was a keen frequenter of coffee bars in his youth – for a while, he and his friends were even known as 'the Kardomah boys'.

Now that Starbucks has taken over the world's coffee bars, the old 'greasy spoons' with their steamed-up windows and communal bowls of white sugar have been mostly forgotten. But not completely; a green plaque marks the site of the 2i's which is known these days as the Boulevard Bar and Dining Room. Very stylish – but it just doesn't have the same ring to it, does it?

# Quiz of the month

All these events took place in the month of February over the past 60 years, but can you arrange them in the order that they happened?

PIC: REX FEATURES

**A** Two 10-year-old boys have been charged with the abduction and murder of two-year-old James Bulger in Liverpool.

**B** The Prince of Wales and the Lady Diana Spencer have ended months of speculation with the announcement they are to be married.

**C** The Kuwaiti capital has been liberated by the Gulf War Allies after 208 days of Iraqi occupation.

**D** The British Conservative Party has chosen Margaret Thatcher as its new leader following a landslide victory over the other four, male, candidates.

**E** Soviets launch the world's biggest space station, Mir, heralding a new phase in space exploration.

**F** Seven Manchester United footballers are among 21 dead after their plane caught fire shortly after take off from Munich.

**G** Scientists in Scotland have announced the birth of the world's first successfully cloned mammal, Dolly the sheep.

**H** Pioneering budget airliner, Laker Airways, has collapsed owing £270 million to banks and other creditors.

**I** Peace envoy Terry Waite has been kidnapped and imprisoned by Islamic militia in Beirut.

**J** Leading anti-apartheid campaigner Nelson Mandela has been freed from prison in South Africa after 27 years.

**K** Jayne Torvill and Christopher Dean have won Olympic ice-skating gold with a performance of a free dance routine to the music of Ravel's Bolero.

**L** Iranian Muslim leader, Ayatollah Khomeini, has issued a death threat against the author Salman Rushdie over the book Satanic Verses.

**M** Hundreds of people clamour to see the marriage of popstars Lulu and Maurice Gibb of the Bee Gees.

**N** His Majesty, King George VI, has died peacefully in his sleep at Sandringham House.

**O** Children all over Britain have emptied out their piggy-banks, heading straight for the nearest shop as sweets come off ration today.

**P** Cassius Clay beats Sonny Liston to become heavyweight champion of the world

News stories taken from http://news.bbc.co.uk/onthisday/

Answer: N) 1952, O) 1953, F) 1958, P) 1964, M) 1969, D) 1975, B) 1981, H) 1982, K) 1984, E) 1986, I) 1987, L) 1989, J) 1990, C) 1991, A) 1993, G) 1997

# March 2010

Monday
## 1
St David's Day

Tuesday
## 2

Wednesday
## 3

Thursday
## 4

Friday
## 5

Saturday
## 6

Sunday
## 7

Monday
## 8

Tuesday
## 9
Yours Live! Skegness

Wednesday
## 10
Yours Live! Skegness

Thursday
## 11
Yours Live! Skegness

Friday
## 12
Yours Live! Skegness

Saturday
## 13

Sunday
## 14
Mothering Sunday

Monday
## 15

Tuesday
## 16

Wednesday
## 17
St Patrick's Day (Bank Holiday Northern Ireland)

Thursday
## 18

Friday
## 19

Saturday
## 20

Sunday
## 21

Monday
## 22

| Tuesday | Sunday |
|---------|--------|
| 23 | 28 |
| | Palm Sunday |
| | British Summer Time begins |

| Wednesday | Monday |
|-----------|--------|
| 24 | 29 |

| Thursday | Tuesday |
|----------|---------|
| 25 | 30 |

| Friday | Wednesday |
|--------|-----------|
| 26 | 31 |

**Saturday**

**27**

## Poetry corner

# England, my England

I love England so very much,
With its green and gentle touch.
I love the leafy, winding lanes,
Villages with quaint sounding names.

I love our traditions; to us they're unique,
They give us our standing – an air of mystique.
I love the habit of afternoon tea,
It's so convivial you see.

I love village fêtes and that sort of thing,
And the sonorous sound of church bell's ring.
I love our Royal pageantry,
And its mark of solidarity.

I love towering cliffs standing guard by our shores,
And the booming sound of the ocean's roar.
I love the way we all hang together,
In times of stress and stormy weather.

I love our climate; although it's perverse,
It gets people talking and could be much worse.
I love north, south, east and west,
For England is home, and home's always best.
**Mrs S Dolby, Sawston, Cambridge**

# Friends forever

I was evacuated with my parents to Shepton Mallet, the home of Babycham. We were billeted with Mr and Mrs Arthur Showering – one of four Showering brothers, who in those days owned a large factory producing beer and cider – the Babycham came later.

Having come from a little terraced house in Barnet, North London, we found ourselves in a huge 300-year-old property called Greathouse, reputed to have belonged to the last Abbot of Glastonbury. Opposite my bedroom was an old rustic door leading to the attic room. At night it was rather scary for a seven-year-old girl. But what treasures it held during the day. Mrs Showering had a trunk up there full of her wonderful oil paintings – it fascinated me.

Often when Mr and Mrs Showering were attending an important function they would slip into my bedroom so that I could gaze wide-eyed at her beautiful evening dresses. I had never seen an evening dress until I was evacuated and no one I knew wore make-up.

Being rather shy I was dreading having to start at a new school, but I was told to look out for a little girl with chestnut coloured ringlets named Joy – the daughter of a colleague of my father's. She was easy to spot in the playground and we began a friendship which has lasted 68 years. In 1966 Joy emigrated with her husband to New Zealand. We've always kept in touch and last year we were able to go and visit her for the first time since she left England – it was a wonderful reunion.

**Gwen Farmer, Seaford, East Sussex**

## Plant profile

## Polyanthus
**Height: 30cm**
**Spread: 15cm**
**Conditions: Thrive in moist soil and sun or partial shade.**

Add instant colour to your early spring garden with polyanthus. A member of the primula family, these plants produce pretty flowers in a kaleidoscopic range of colours atop short upright stems. There are hundreds of varieties to choose from but if you want more than your local garden centre can provide, try Barnhaven Primulas from Sonia Wright's nursery, Buckerfields, near Marlborough in Wiltshire.

## Health tip
### Give back

Retired people who volunteer live longer than those who don't say US researchers. Doing your bit improves your social network and your self esteem, which seems to extend longevity. Contact Volunteering England to find out more. Visit www.volunteering.org.uk

## Senior moment

I attend a club where we pay a small sum each week to cover expenses for our many activities. At a recent meeting I was told, as I had been absent for two meetings, I owed two weeks subscription. I couldn't think why I had been absent until somebody asked if I had enjoyed my holiday in France!

**Olwyn Shaw, Southport**

## Fast fact

Chemist T L Williams made the first mascara from Vaseline petroleum jelly and coal dust for his sister Mabel. Soon the Maybelline brand was formed and its first ever cake mascara flew of the shelves in 1917.

## Small talk

Driving in the car with our grandchildren sitting in the back, Courtney, aged 10, asked where we were going. "Connah's Quay," I replied. Not hearing me, Courtney said: "Pardon," to which her seven-year-old brother, Connor, piped up: "We're going to my key!"

**Christine Hartshorn, Llandudno**

## Fashion we wore

I thought readers might like to see my wedding photographs. We were married March 1946 in Birmingham. It was very cold and there was a sprinkling of snow still on the ground. My husband wore his demob suit because we spent all our clothing coupons on honeymoon clothes for the two of us. My gown was hired, as was one of the bridesmaid's dresses. The other two bridesmaid's dresses were borrowed, one was mine and the other was a friend's. There was one each of pink, blue and lilac, so we dyed the muffs and headdresses to match.

**Irene Robson, Dinas Powys**

# Recipe of the week

## Mushroom En-croûte

Serves 4

- ◆ 375 g (11 oz) pack ready-rolled puff pastry
- ◆ 4 large white flat mushrooms
- ◆ 4 tbsp green pesto
- ◆ 8 sun-dried tomatoes in oil, drained
- ◆ 150 g (6 oz) mozzarella cheese, sliced
- ◆ Milk, to glaze

1. Preheat the oven to 200°C/400°F/Gas Mark 7. Unroll the pastry on a lightly floured surface, then use a rolling pin to lightly roll the pastry so it measures 38 x 32 cm (approx 15 x 12 in) and cut into four pieces. Place a mushroom in the centre of each pastry rectangle.
2. Top each mushroom with a tablespoon of pesto, 2 tomatoes and slices of mozzarella. Season well.
3. Brush the pastry edges with milk and bring the corners up and over the topping and press to seal together.
4. Place onto a large baking tray and brush all over with milk. Bake for 20-25 mins, or until the pastry is golden brown. Serve immediately with boiled new potatoes and vegetables.

◆ **Top Tip:** These can be prepared up to 48 hours in advance, unglazed and wrapped in clingfilm.

Recipe: Mushroom Bureau, www.mushroom-uk.com

# When disaster struck

June and her husband strike a dance pose

My late husband and I were very keen senior novice old-time and sequence ballroom dancers. We had successfully qualified in regional heats for a Novice of the Year competition, and if we won this we'd lose our novice status and would become Pre-Champion dancers. When we arrived at the ballroom in Birmingham, it looked splendid. A huge silver ball hung from the ceiling spinning a rainbow of colours. My husband looked very handsome in his midnight-blue tail suit, white shirt, bow tie, gloves and shiny black shoes. I wore a beautiful pink sequinned dress, which lay shimmering on top of a very full pink petticoat made of yards and yards of tulle net. There we stood in this wonderful ballroom, full of music, lights and dancers. I'll never forget how nervous I felt.

The first rounds of the competition had been danced and the twelve couples chosen for the semi-final, us included, had just finished dancing. The atmosphere was electric as we all waited with bated breath for the final six of the Novice Competition of the year to be announced. There was a deathly hush as the compère took to the stage to announce the final six. To our delight our number was called amid clapping and cheers. My husband took my hand and we proudly took our places on the dance floor with the other five competitors. The first dance was a waltz followed by the tango. It was going well, when disaster struck. Halfway through the last dance I could feel my under skirt slipping down! We continued dancing but, as I spun a perfect spin, down came my underskirt. I fled off the stage amid wolf-whistles and laughter. To this day I still don't know if our sixth position was awarded because of my falling underskirt or our dancing! We did eventually loose our Novice status.

**June Davenport, Shropshire**

## Plant profile

### Primrose

**Height: 15cm**

**Spread: 15cm**

**Conditions: Thrives in moist soil in sun or partial shade. Great in borders, baskets and containers.**

Loved by all, the native primrose produces clusters of single yellow flowers in early spring and can be seen on grassy banks across the countryside. So many hybrids have been produced that you can now enjoy plants with flowers in every colour imaginable. Deadhead regularly to encourage more flowers and, once they've finished blooming, move them to a shady corner of the garden. Available from garden centres.

## Health tip
### Fit not fat

Make getting fit your health goal this week rather than burning fat. People over 60 who are physically fit and stay active live longer than their unfit friends, regardless of their body fat say US scientists. The good news is getting fit will help you to lose weight too.

## Senior moment

I asked my mum if she was watching the new TV programme that featured Anton Du Beke. She immediately said: "No, I don't like those two Geordie lads." It took me a few seconds to realise she meant Ant and Dec!

**Marian Illingworth, Musselburgh**

## Fast fact

Concorde made its maiden test flight on March 2, 1969. Although Concorde's speed didn't rise above 300mph on this first flight – it would later reach speeds of 1300 mph. The first commercial flight took place in January 1976 and the last commercial flight was in October 2003.

## Small talk

I was babysitting overnight for my granddaughter, aged three. When she found out she said to her Mum: "I don't want to stay the night at Grandma's, but I'll go and play with her."
**Ms D Scott, Sailsbury**

## Fashion we wore

This photo shows me and Sheila (right), off on our first trip on our own to London. We were going to the Sunday Pictorial Star Garden Party, meeting stars such as Valerie Hobson, Dirk Bogarde, Cesar Romero and many more. When we arrived there was quite a queue forming outside the venue. When the gates opened everyone rushed forward leaving us behind, but as we had tickets we got in eventually anyway. We're both wearing our 'New Look' coats, mine was a wine colour and Sheila's was bottle green.
**Pamela Pilbeam, Herne Bay, Kent**

## Recipe of the week

### Steamed ginger sponge
Serves 6

**For the sponge:**
- 175 g (7 oz) unsalted butter, softened
- 2 large eggs, beaten
- 170 g (7 oz) tube Carnation Condensed Milk
- 225 g (9 oz) self-raising flour
- ½ tsp baking powder
- 75 g (3 oz) stem ginger in syrup, drained and finely chopped

**For the syrup:**
- 100 g (4 oz) icing sugar
- 200 ml (8 fl oz) water
- 50 g (2 oz) pieces of stem ginger, roughly chopped
- 2 tbsp stem ginger syrup
- 2 tbsp orange jelly marmalade (without peel)
- Finely chopped zest and juice of a medium orange

1. Preheat the oven to 180°C/350°F/Gas Mark 4 and lightly grease a 1.5 litre (2½ pt) ovenproof dish.
2. In a large mixing bowl, place all the sponge ingredients, except the stem ginger, and whisk until smooth and pale. Gently fold in the ginger and spoon into the dish. Place in a large roasting tin and fill the tin with enough boiling water to come two-thirds up the sides of the dish. Bake for 45 minutes, or until risen and golden brown.
3. Meanwhile, make the syrup. Using a small saucepan, bring all the syrup ingredients, except the orange zest, to the boil. Boil for 5–10 minutes, or until the mixture has slightly thickened.
4. Remove from the heat and stir in the orange zest. Pour the syrup over the warm sponge. Serve immediately with crème fraîche, or with lashings of warm custard.
Recipe: Nestlé Carnation, www.carnation.co.uk

# Daddy's girl

Shirley and her dad Victor

When I was younger I was definitely a daddy's girl. My father had come to Great Britain during the war after fighting in the Polish army. We loved spending quality time together and mum must have been a bit jealous at times as we would spend hours just chatting. His stories of the war always fascinated me and, in particular, how he had escaped from Germany with the help of the French Resistance.

A non-smoker in my lifetime he always said smoking had saved his life. He'd been dropped into Germany by parachute to act as a spy for the allied forces. His cover story centred on him being German but living near the Polish border hence his accent. My father spoke fluent Polish, German and English – a bilingual talent I didn't inherit. He was to report on the movement of munitions and troops and radio back details to enable bombing raids to be targeted. This he did successfully with a colleague at night, while during the day he worked in a German factory. One day he stopped to buy some cigarettes from a shop, but his friend, who didn't smoke waited outside. My father looked out of the shop window in time to see his friend being bundled into the back of a Gestapo car. He later learnt his friend had been shot as a spy so, in effect, smoking saved his life. My father went on the run and contacted the French Resistance who helped him escape to Switzerland. This story and others will always remind me of his bravery and of a terrific dad.

**Shirley O'Neill, Peterborough**

## Plant profile

### Eranthus Hyemalis

**Height: 13cm**
**Spread: 10cm**
**Conditions: Enjoys well-drained soil and a shady position.**

A charming woodland plant with cup-shaped yellow flowers, E hyemalis looks wonderful when allowed to naturalise under deciduous trees, Spreading quickly to produce a carpet of gold. It has an Award of Garden Merit from the RHS. Widely available as bulbs from garden centres during the autumn or online from specialist suppliers such as www.dejager.co.uk

## Health tip
### Are you getting enough?

If you're over 65 you should be getting a minimum of 1,300 mg of calcium everyday according to the World Health Organisation. Calcium is found in dairy products, green leafy vegetables, canned sardines and other fish you eat with bones and dried fruits. If you don't think you're getting enough take a supplement.

## Senior moment

I came home from shopping, brewed a small pot of tea and put some potatoes in the pressure cooker. After waiting for it to brew I was surprised when I poured the tea and got a cup of hot, clear water. I opened the pressure cooker – lovely brown potatoes – Yorkshire Tea flavour!

**Valerie Howard, Hawick**

## Fast fact

No piece of paper can be folded squarely in half more than seven times. Go on try it now! The size of the paper doesn't matter but you must fold the paper in half, turn it 90° then in half again, and so on. It gets really tricky after six folds.

## Small talk

I liked to think that my four-year-old grandson thought of me as 'bright and breezy'. But I'm not so sure since I heard him announcing: "My grandma, she's old and draughty."

**Mrs S Lane, Devon**

## Fashion we wore

**H**ere are two wedding photos, which I thought readers might like to see. The first is of my maternal grandparents' wedding day in 1925. The bride and groom are Edith and William Knott, in the centre of the picture. The lady on the far right is William's sister, Jessie, but I'm afraid I don't know the names of the other people. The other wedding photo (below) is that of my parents, Ron and Barbara Bailey, on January 20, 1949. Dad's parents are behind him on the left and mum's parents (Edith and William) are behind her on the right.

**Christine Barrow, Plymouth**

## Recipe of the week

### Raisin and cinnamon eggy bread
**Serves 4**

◆ 2-3 tbsp sunflower or vegetable oil
◆ 4 large Lion eggs
◆ 6 slices raisin and cinnamon loaf
◆ 100 g (4 oz) fresh blueberries and raspberries
◆ 4 tbsp crème fraîche, to serve

1. Heat a little of the oil in a non-stick frying pan. Beat the eggs in a shallow dish. Dip 2-3 slices of the raisin bread into the beaten egg, turning until fully coated.
2. Cook them in the hot oil for 4-5 minutes, or until golden brown on both sides.
3. Transfer these to a plate and keep warm. Repeat with the remaining egg and bread.
4. Cut the eggy bread slices in half diagonally and arrange 3 pieces per person onto 4 plates. Scatter over the raspberries and blueberries, and serve immediately with a tablespoon of crème fraîche on each plate.

Recipe: British Lion Eggs, www.eggrecipes.co.uk

# Our wedding day

Betty and her husband Bill on their wedding day

**R**ecently my friends and I were discussing the credit crunch and the effect it would have on the cost of a certain granddaughter's wedding. My thoughts strayed back sixty-three years to my own wedding when it all seemed much simpler as we didn't know the cost.

I was demobbed in February 1946 and Bill in March. He had a job to return to and his boss wanted him to start as soon as possible, so we decided to get married by the end of the same month. My parents arranged the wedding and at no time did we consider the cost. My mother contacted the Food Office for the additional coupons for such occasions. She altered my sister Bernice's wedding dress and fortunately the bridesmaid dress that I wore to Bernice's wedding fitted Bill's sister, who was to be my bridesmaid. The reception was held at my parent's house and mother used a plank over chairs to allow more people to sit at the table. Unfortunately, she didn't realise that people's bottoms were bigger than the spaces that she had planned. This meant my brother Tony and his girlfriend had to sit at the bottom of the stairs!

After a happy meal we made our way to the railway station where we were waved off on a train to London. To this day I have never known the cost, or the trouble, involved – how different things are today.

**Betty Baxter, Liverpool**

## Plant profile

### Hyacinth 'Carnegie'
**Height: 30cm**
**Spread: 15cm**
**Conditions: Plant in well-drained soil in sun or partial shade, or in containers of moist bulb fibre.**
The enticing scent of the hyacinth is hard to beat. Named after Hyakinthos, a handsome young man from Greek mythology, they're one of the first plants to bloom in spring and are great as bedding or in containers, positioned where you can enjoy their scent. Buy 'heat-treated' bulbs in autumn – these will flower early at Christmas. Alternatively, plant outside for flowers in early spring.

## Health tip
### Head off headaches

If you feel a headache or a migraine coming on get on your bike. A study in the journal Headache found that regular exercise such as cycling helped to reduce the frequency and ease the severity of headaches and migraines.

## Senior moment

Early one morning I went shopping in our local supermarket. I collected my trolley and thought how nice and quiet it was. It was only when I got to the checkout I was told that the store didn't open for another half an hour. So I had to leave my shopping and wait until it did!

**Thora May, Kent**

## Fast fact

The Eiffel Tower has 1,665 steps in the East Pillar to the very top and stands at 324 metres in height. It was originally planned to be torn down in 1909, but was saved when radio arrived and it was used as a transmitter. It draws an average of 10,000 visitors a day.

## Small talk

My four-year-old grandson Damon came to lunch. On seeing I had displayed his first school photo he said: "Why aren't I smiling? They must have bent my mouth straight."

**Fran Norris, Plymouth**

## Fashion we wore

**H**ere's a picture of me in my back garden in March 1963, just before I set off to a friend's wedding. I was all of 18 years old at the time and it was a cold March morning – the snow had just cleared following a very long icy winter. The wool suit I'm wearing was light blue and I bought it from a shop in Petticoat Lane for £10 (£5 down, then 10s a week for it). The white faux-fur bowler hat was bought from a local hat manufacturer in Essex. I wore a crisp white blouse with black gloves, bag and black patent shoes with buckles that matched the buckles on my bag. We had a lovely day and I felt I was the bee's knees at the time.

**Bobbie Jones, South Benfleet, Essex**

## Recipe of the week

### Cherry and walnut hot cross buns
**Makes 12**

◆ 500 g (20 oz) premium white bread mix
◆ Zest 1 lemon
◆ 2 tsp caster sugar
◆ 2 tsp ground mixed spice
◆ 150 ml (½ pt) warm milk
◆ 2 large Lion eggs
◆ 25 g (1 oz) butter, melted
◆ 75 g (3 oz) currants
◆ 75 g (3 oz) glacé cherries, quartered
◆ 50 g (2 oz) walnut pieces, chopped
◆ A little milk to glaze
◆ 4 tbsp plain flour
◆ 2 tbsp clear honey

1. Preheat the oven to 200°C/400°F/Gas Mark 7.
2. In a large mixing bowl, add the bread mix, lemon zest, sugar and spice. Place the milk in a measuring jug, add the eggs and beat well. Make up to 300 ml (1 pt) with warm water. Stir into the dry ingredients before adding the butter, currants, cherries and walnuts.
3. Mix well with your hands and turn out onto a floured surface. Knead for 5 minutes, or until the dough is smooth and elastic. Leave to rest for 5 minutes.
4. Further knead for 2 minutes, before dividing into 12 pieces. Shape each piece into a flattish round and place on a lightly greased baking sheet. Brush the tops with a little milk. Score a cross in the centre of each and leave to prove in a warm place until doubled in size.
5. In a small bowl, mix the flour with 3 tablespoons of cold water to form a smooth paste. Then pipe into the crosses formed on top of the buns. Bake for 20-25 minutes, or until golden brown.
6. Remove and immediately brush with the honey. Leave to cool on the baking sheet for 5 minutes before transferring to a wire rack. Serve warm with butter.

British Lion Eggs, www.eggrecipes.co.uk

# I remember the Festival of Britain

## BY: MARION CLARKE

'A tonic for the nation' was how Labour MP Herbert Morrison described the 1951 Festival of Britain. And with London and other major cities still scarred by bomb sites and food rationing an everyday reality, we were certainly in need of cheering up.

The Government allocated a budget of £8 million to demolishing run-down terraces and warehouses on the South Bank of the Thames to make way for new constructions that included the Royal Festival Hall, the futuristic Skylon tower and the Dome of Discovery (a forerunner of the Millennium Dome in Greenwich). Also included in the attractions were the Festival Pleasure Gardens in Battersea which featured a tree walk, a fun fair and the much admired Guinness Clock on which characters from the Guinness adverts performed a routine four times an hour.

## We were certainly in need of cheering up

Outside London, there were festivals in places such as Cardiff, Perth, York and Cheltenham. The village of Trowell in Northamptonshire was chosen to be the Festival Village, a typical example of rural life.

The ambitious project was not without its critics who felt that with many people still living in prefabs the money would be better spent on housing. Its defendants pointed to the public housing estate in Poplar that the Festival built to demonstrate modern town planning ideas. Named the Lansbury Estate, it had its own pub and church, and is still standing today.

Of the new buildings on the South Bank, only the Festival Hall remains – the other constructions were pulled down when a new government came into power in 1953. The incoming Prime Minister, Winston Churchill, considered them to be too 'socialist' in style.

Despite the controversy surrounding it, the Festival proved to be hugely popular and even made a profit. Thousands of people visited it between May and September 1951 and many of their memories have been recorded by the Museum of London

PIC: GETTY IMAGES

The Festival of Britain divided opinions but those who visited the London site have vivid memories of it.

which held an exhibition of the Festival in 2001 (visit website www.museumoflondon.org.uk). Michael Wontner-Riches has written: "My parents took me to the Festival of Britain soon after its opening. We were living in Greenford Middlesex and I have clear memories of that visit, seeing the Skylon and the Dome of Discovery. While there my father bought me a George VI Crown which we watched being minted on the South Bank site by the Royal Mint. I still have that coin, still in its original claret coloured box."

Another visitor to the exhibition recalled: "I lived in a terraced street in Custom House, the docklands East End of London. The Festival to me at the age of five years consisted of a street party with bunting and Union Jacks everywhere which was all very exciting!"

A tonic indeed!

# Quiz of the month

All these events took place in the month of March over the past 60 years, but can you arrange them in the order that they happened?

PIC REX FEATURES

**F** Nationalist leader Robert Mugabe has won a sweeping election victory to become Zimbabwe's first black prime minister.

**G** Notorious gangland killer Ronnie Kray has died in hospital two days after he collapsed at Broadmoor where he was serving a life sentence for murder.

**H** Former Yugoslav President Slobodan Milosevic has been arrested and taken to prison, ending a heavily armed standoff at his Belgrade villa.

**I** Buckingham Palace has announced that Princess Margaret and Lord Snowdon are to separate after 16 years of marriage.

**J** Silent film legend Charlie Chaplin has become Sir Charles after a ceremony at Buckingham Palace.

**K** Tens of thousands of Britain's miners have stopped work in what looks set to become a long-running battle against job losses.

**A** An anti poll-tax rally in central London has erupted into the worst riots seen in the city for a century. Forty-five police officers are among the 113 people injured.

**B** Forty-nine people have been confirmed dead and dozens are missing after a car ferry capsized just outside the Belgian port of Zeebrugge.

**C** Jack Ruby has been sentenced to death after being found guilty of the murder of Lee Harvey Oswald, the alleged assassin of President John F Kennedy.

**D** Large parts of the British railway system are declared uneconomic in Dr Beeching's report.

**E** Mikhail Gorbachev is the new man in charge at the Kremlin, having taken over following the death of Konstantin Chernenko.

**L** The disgraced Olympic sprinter, Ben Johnson, has been banned from athletics for life after failing a drugs test for a second time.

**M** The Exxon Valdez oil tanker has run aground on a reef off the Alaskan coast, releasing gallons of crude oil into the sea.

**N** The supersonic airliner, Concorde, makes a 'faultless' maiden flight.

**O** The US has produced the biggest ever man-made explosion when they tested the hydrogen bomb on the Pacific archipelago of Bikini.

**P** Thousands of people have jogged through the normally quiet Sunday streets of the capital to compete in the first ever London marathon.

News stories taken from http://news.bbc.co.uk/onthisday/

Answer: O) 1954, D) 1963, C) 1964, N) 1969, J) 1975, I) 1976, F) 1980, P) 1981, K) 1984, E) 1985, B) 1987, M) 1989, A) 1990, L) 1993, G) 1995, H) 2001.

# Tomorrow we diet

## BY: ELIZABETH MOULDER

### A visit from cousin Mandy stretches Shelley's willpower to breaking point

"Shelley, guess what?" her mum asked. "I'm too hungry for guessing games. What's for tea?" Gloria opened the fridge. "Cottage cheese, tofu, some wilted lettuce, one yoghurt and left-over chicken."

"I suppose a quick trip to the chippie is out of the question?"

"Yes it is! We've got to be strong. It's weigh-in tomorrow and we both gained last week. I'll do something with the chicken, but let's have a cup of tea first – I want to tell you about Mandy."

"Cousin Mandy?"

"Your Aunty Sylvia rang, Mandy's moving here to start training for the fire service. Sylvia wondered if she could stay with us until she gets a flat."

"Well, we don't mind, if it's just temporary."

## "Come in. I wouldn't have known you."

"It's your room she'll be sharing. But I'm not changing our diet. It's a month to our holiday and I've got another half stone to lose."

"We'll manage. It's ages since we saw her last. She was a podgy little thing then, with spots. When is she coming?"

"Day after tomorrow. Now, about that chicken…"

Two days later, Gloria flung open the door and greeted her niece: "Mandy! Come in. I wouldn't have known you. Put your bags down and I'll make tea. You remember Shelley?"

"Hi, Mandy!" Shelley gasped before swiftly following Gloria into the kitchen.

She whispered: "She's drop dead gorgeous! Slim as a rail and skin like a peach. I wonder what diet she's on?"

"Ask her. Hold the door, will you?"

"Sorry I can't offer you a biscuit, Mandy. We don't buy them – too much temptation."

"That's all right, Aunty G. I bought these for the journey." Diving into her handbag, she produced a packet of chocolate digestives. "Help yourselves. Is there any sugar?"

"I'll get it," muttered Shelley.

"You've changed since we last saw you, Mandy," said Gloria.

"I expect I was fat then," said Mandy, cheerfully.

"What did you do?" asked Shelley, plonking the sugar bowl down. "Weight Watchers? Slimming World? Atkins?"

"No, I suddenly got taller and the fat disappeared. Just as well, I love my food."

"We're dieting," said Gloria. "We want to look good for our holiday. You might not like what we eat."

"We don't even like it," said Shelley, with feeling.

"Don't worry. I'll be eating at the fire station most of the time."

Shelley and Gloria were picking at their baked potatoes with cottage cheese the next evening when the door banged and Mandy sailed in with a steaming, fragrant parcel.

"Evening all," she smiled. "I passed your local chippie and couldn't resist. Chip anyone?"

Gloria swallowed. "No, we're fine," she said, faintly. "Maybe just one?" pleaded Shelley.

"No, Shell. We've got to be firm."

"You don't know what you're missing," said Mandy as her perfect teeth sank into the crisp, glistening batter. "You are lucky to have such a good chippie at the end of your road."

"We know," said Shelley. "We used to go there every Friday night."

"And that's why we've got to diet now," Gloria reminded her.

The next night Mandy arrived with cream doughnuts. "Help yourselves. One can't hurt."

"She picks all our favourite things – chocolate digestives, chips and cream doughnuts," hissed Shelley over the washing up. "Is she doing it on purpose?"

"She doesn't mean any harm. When you've never dieted in your life you just don't understand. We'll give it till the weekend and then I'll say something."

PIC: KATE DAVIES

# "I can't believe I ate all the popcorn..."

"Great film, this!" Mandy waltzed in, waving a DVD. "I thought we could have a girls' night in. And you can't have a proper girls' night in without – da-da!"

Gloria and Shelley groaned as out came a bottle of wine, popcorn and chocolates.

"I'll get some diet coke and a bag of no-fat crisps for us," Shelley said, hurriedly.

"Shame!" said Mandy. "Where's the corkscrew?"

Later, Mandy stretched and yawned: "Wasn't that a great evening? I can't believe I ate ALL the popcorn AND the chocolates."

Shelley said, tensely: "Mum wants to ask you something."

"Does she? Oh, before I forget – I'll be moving out tomorrow. It's been fun here with you two but I have to go, really."

"I'll help you pack," said Shelley, helpfully.

Wreathed in smiles, they waved Mandy goodbye.

"That was more than flesh and blood should have to bear," said Gloria.

"It was cruel," agreed Shelley. "I'm off for a bit of retail therapy. I'll bring something back for lunch."

"Right. See you at one o'clock."

Gloria and Shell arrived home at the same time. Shelley walked into the kitchen, clutching a steaming, fragrant parcel and a bottle of wine.

"I'm sorry, Mum," she said. "But after what we've been through, we deserve these. Get the salt and vinegar."

Sighing happily, Gloria unwrapped the fish and chips. "You're right, Shell," she said. "I don't know how we resisted all that temptation, night after night."

They ate in silent appreciation, relishing each perfect chip, crunching delicately each forkful of battered fish.

Replete, they sat back. Gloria raised her glass: "To absent friends."

"And may the thin ones stay absent," said Shelley. "Gosh, I'm full. I don't think I'll eat again for a week."

"That's a pity," said Gloria, pulling out a carrier bag. "Because I've got cream doughnuts for afters."

"You know, if you eat a month's calories all in one day, it sort of spreads itself out, and doesn't really count. I'm sure I read that somewhere. Shall we finish off that bottle before we have the doughnuts?"

| Thursday | | Monday | |
|---|---|---|---|
| **1** | Maundy Thursday | **12** | |

| Friday | | Tuesday | |
|---|---|---|---|
| **2** | Good Friday | **13** | |

| Saturday | | Wednesday | |
|---|---|---|---|
| **3** | | **14** | |

| Sunday | | Thursday | |
|---|---|---|---|
| **4** | Easter Sunday | **15** | |

| Monday | | Friday | |
|---|---|---|---|
| **5** | Easter Monday | **16** | |

| Tuesday | | Saturday | |
|---|---|---|---|
| **6** | | **17** | |

| Wednesday | | Sunday | |
|---|---|---|---|
| **7** | | **18** | |

| Thursday | | Monday | |
|---|---|---|---|
| **8** | | **19** | |

| Friday | | Tuesday | |
|---|---|---|---|
| **9** | | **20** | |

| Saturday | | Wednesday | |
|---|---|---|---|
| **10** | | **21** | Queen Elizabeth's Birthday |

| Sunday | | Thursday | |
|---|---|---|---|
| **11** | | **22** | |

| Friday | | Tuesday |
|---|---|---|
| **23** | St George's Day | **27** |
| Saturday | | Wednesday |
| **24** | | **28** |
| Sunday | | Thursday |
| **25** | London Marathon | **29** |
| Monday | | Friday |
| **26** | | **30** |

## Poetry corner

# Spring clean

We're turning out some junk to make some extra space,
Boxed up all old videos and some you can't replace.
We put them in the garden and now we're on old clothes,
We sort though them all – no, we won't need those.

Then come old books – some we've never even read,
Bung them in the box and take 'em up the tip instead.
Then the funny gadgets – electric hand held whisk,
That daft fondue set and all the dipping sticks.

The house is empty now of all things we might need,
We have worked hard on this – it's been a struggle indeed.
We couldn't chuck them out though, so we stored them instead,
The only problem now is, we can't get in the shed.

**Andrea Hazeldine, Middlesex**

# Working for the Co-op

Edna in her scooter gear with her colleagues from the Co-op

I left school in July 1957 at the age of 15 and started my first job at the Co-op just two weeks later. At this time Leyland was a small, but very industrious village with Leyland Motors being the main employer. The Leyland & Farington Co-operative Society Ltd was a large grocery business with eight grocery branches, a ladies clothing shop, a butchers shop and a coal yard, with two offices above a large drapery store. They also had their own garage across from the drapery store to repair the company vehicles.

Bert, who worked in the boardroom in the daytime, serviced and repaired the vehicles in the garage at night. I was 18 years old when I took my driving test in 1960 – dressed all in white looking like an advert for washing powder! My ex-boyfriend kindly lent his scooter to me to take my test as this was before I had bought my own. I passed first time and everyone at the Co-op was very proud of me. Sadly it was never the same after Preston Co-op amalgamated with Leyland Co-op in the early Sixties. I still see some of my old work colleagues when I'm out shopping and we often talk about the fun we had at the Co-op. We all say it was the best job we ever had.

**Edna Lydiate, Leyland**

## Plant profile

### Viola 'Moonbeam'

**Height: 15cm**
**Spread: 15cm**
**Conditions: Thrives in moist, well-drained soil and sun or partial shade.**

Violas add colour all summer long, with cheery little 'faces' that are hard to resist. Great as bedding, in hanging baskets or in containers, they have universal appeal. Water and feed them regularly and deadhead the blooms as they fade and they'll continue flowering well into November. This variety produces loads of pastel blue flowers all summer and is available as seed from www.nickys-nursery.co.uk

## Health tip

### Go dark

Protect your heart as you indulge by opting for dark chocolate Easter eggs with a minimum of 70 per cent cocoa solids. The antioxidants in lovely, dense, dark chocolate are thought to prevent damage to your arteries and in turn protect your heart.

## Senior moment

In the middle of ironing, I stepped away for a moment to open the kitchen windows. On returning, I picked up the kettle by mistake and poured water all over the ironing board and the shirt which I was about to iron! **Maureen Hamilton, Dudley**

## Fast fact

Heathrow Airport was taken over by the Ministry of Civil Aviation and officially opened in 1946 with a tented terminal. A new terminal building replaced the tent in the early Fifties. Today Heathrow is the UK's largest airport carrying over 68 million passengers each year.

## Small talk

Seeing a trail of white smoke from a plane in the sky, I heard a little boy say to his Mum: "Look Mum, someone's going to see Jesus." **Sue Beck, Plymouth**

## Fashion we wore

This is a picture of my friend and I taken in spring 1957 outside the wedding reception of a mutual friend? I'm on the right and Mildred Petrie is on the left. Mildred's outfit is an emerald green suit with a 'sunray' pleated skirt and white accessories. My coat was pure wool, in a camel shade, with a big shawl collar. I am wearing a small red, feathered hat and a red dress. We both had gloves and boxy handbags, which were the fashion. Mildred and I are still good friends and live just 16 miles apart.

**Mary Reynard, Barnsley**

## Recipe of the week

### Chocolate Easter torte
**Serves 12**

- 100 g (4 oz) butter, softened
- 100 g (4 oz) light soft brown sugar
- 100 g (4 oz) ground almonds
- 4 large Lion Quality eggs, separated
- 50 g (2 oz) fresh, brown breadcrumbs
- 150 g (6 oz) plain chocolate, melted
- 225 g (9 oz) marzipan
- 4 tbsp apricot jam, melted
- 200 g (8 oz) plain chocolate
- 200 ml (8 fl oz) double cream
- 12 foil-wrapped mini chocolate eggs

1. Preheat the oven to 180°C/350°F/Gas Mark 4. Grease a 23 cm (9 inch) loose-bottomed cake tin and line the base.
2. In a large bowl, mix the butter and sugar until light and fluffy. Stir in the almonds, egg yolks, breadcrumbs and melted chocolate. In a separate bowl, whisk the egg whites until stiff and fold into the mixture.
3. Spoon into the tin and bake for 40-45 minutes. Remove from the oven and cover the cake with a damp tea towel and leave to cool in the tin. Turn out onto a wire rack.
4. Roll out the marzipan and cut out a 23 cm (9 inch) circle. Cut the cake in half horizontally, brush the cut surfaces with the jam, place the marzipan between and sandwich together. Brush the rest of the jam all over.
5. In a small saucepan, melt the chocolate and cream together. Leave to cool slightly to thicken.
6. Put the cake onto a serving plate. Completely cover the cake with the chocolate icing and leave to cool before decorating with the mini eggs.

Recipe: British Lion Eggs, www.eggrecipes.co.uk

# An eventful walk

**M**any years ago I was walking my two dogs in the park with my mum. A large dog appeared and started being very aggressive towards my two. My Springer Spaniel, Major, tried to protect Sophie, our other dog, but it was clear he was coming off a lot worse and was on his back with the other dog over him going for his throat.

Without thinking I stepped in (something you should never do) and grabbed the dog by its throat and squeezed gently but firmly. It was just the right pressure to make the dog freeze. It all went quiet and Major jumped up off his back safely. I let the other dog go and he calmly walked off as if nothing had happened.

Major and Sophie relaxing after their adventure

My mum asked: "How did you know how to do that?" I had no idea – I didn't think – I just acted instinctively. Now if I tried to do that again I would get the timing wrong and would probably get bitten by the dog. It's a puzzle and something I hope never happens again, but memorable nonetheless.

**Alan Cosgrove, London**

## Plant profile

### Bellis Perennis

**Height: 15cm**
**Spread: 15cm**
**Conditions: Thrives in well -drained compost in sun or partial shade.**

A close relative of the common daisy, this charming plant is great as spring bedding. There are numerous varieties to choose between with red, purple or white pompom flowers and all look superb in baskets, containers or at the front of a border. Although perennial in habit, it's best grown as an annual and used to provide extra splashes of colour during the spring. Plants are widely available from garden centres.

## Health tip
### Meditate

If you're after a bigger, stronger brain then it's time to meditate. Scientists from UCLA found that people who meditate have stronger brains and are more capable of being positive, emotionally stable and mindful. Set aside 10 minutes each day to sit quietly and clear your mind.

## Senior moment

While shopping early one morning with my husband we decided to have breakfast. When it came, my husband shook the salt liberally over it but then realised it was the sugar. He then ate the lot and said it was the sweetest breakfast he'd ever had.

**Margaret Westwood, Staffs**

## Fast fact

Every year in the UK around £8.5 billion of energy is wasted. And each household creates six tonnes of carbon dioxide – enough to fill a hot air balloon, according to the Energy Saving Trust. The average householder could save around 1.5 tonnes of carbon dioxide (CO2) every year by making their home more energy efficient.

## Small talk

My niece, Ellen, is always making us laugh, especially when at a farm she announced: "I've just seen a whole pig!"

**Mrs Giblin, South Wales**

## Fashion we wore

This photo shows me and my friends arriving in Illfracombe on a day trip. It was 1949 and we all worked at the Smith's Watch Company in Ystradgywlais in the Swansea Valley. We crossed the Bristol Channel and the sea was very rough, but the sailors made us welcome with bacon sarnies!

I'm the one on the far right carrying a case. My shoulder bag and shoes were leather, made by a local cobbler. Our dresses were the latest fashion. This new length had just come in and the style was to have a white background and colourful patterns. I remember mine had mushrooms, of all things, on the border and it cost me £2 10s.

**Margaret Esme Evans, Neath**

## Recipe of the week

## Oak-smoked ham & pepper frittata
### Serves 2

- ◆ 250 g (10 oz) small new potatoes
- ◆ 1 tbsp Rapeseed Oil
- ◆ 1 red pepper, diced
- ◆ 75 g (3 oz) oak-smoked ham, diced
- ◆ 4 medium eggs, beaten
- ◆ 2 tbsp semi-skimmed milk

1. In a saucepan, boil the potatoes for 10 minutes, or until tender. Run under cold water then slice thickly. Preheat the grill to a medium heat.
2. Meanwhile, in a 24 cm (9 inch) frying pan, heat the oil and fry the pepper for 2 minutes. Add the sliced potatoes and fry for a further 1-2 minutes before adding the ham.
3. In a small mixing bowl, blend the eggs and milk together and season well. Pour into the frying pan. Cook gently for 3 minutes, loosening the edges with a spatula.
4. Grill for 3 minutes, or until golden brown and completely set.
5. Serve immediately with a fresh green salad.

Recipe: Rapeseed Oil, www.hgca.com

# One for the ladies

Andy Wade and Hazel Cleaver who was Miss Britain In 1956

In the late Seventies, as audiences in clubs started to diminish, another vogue of entertainment surfaced called the hen-party – the women's equivalent to male stag parties. A fellow performer of mine called Andy Wade, who was also a 'physical culturist', was among the earliest innovators of this risqué act, in which men stripped off their clothes instead of women.

Reading about Andy's antics in a national newspaper inspired a friend to leave his boring office job and follow in his footsteps. Since then he never looked back – what a lovely way of earning a living, making hundreds of women happy each night, instead of one! It was suggested that our act might go down well as hen-party entertainment. Well it certainly did and I've still got the scars to prove it.

As we walked on to the floor of one pub we were greeted with voracious 'oohs and aahs' and later when we finished our act, a woman jumped up and ran her finger nails down my arm. Later Andy told us about the 'eight o'clock woman' who arrives at the party, mildly inquisitive and sober, but as the night wears on she gradually begins to get more tipsy, until she turns into the 'ten o'clock woman'. By the time the male stripper comes on, she is baying and yelling 'get 'em off'. Thankfully our modesty was covered at all times and most of the time we did our act before the eight o'clock woman turned into the ten o'clock one!

**Bob Sterling, Stourbridge**

## Plant profile

### Magnolia Soulangeana

**Height: 5m**
**Spread: 5m**
**Conditions: Magnolias prefer well-drained, slightly acidic soils and do well in sun or partial shade.**

Position is everything. Magnolias are a class act and with stylish, fragrant flowers demand a prime location. Sadly, their flowers can be damaged by frost, so it's only worth growing a magnolia as a specimen if your garden's sheltered from the elements. If your plot's more exposed, choose a woodland setting as this will give them more protection and, if you want extra colour, underplant with spring-flowering bulbs.

## Health tip

### Get more vitamin C

Not only is vitamin C a good immune booster it could help to reduce your risk of gout too. Researchers found that getting between 1,000 and 1,500mg of vitamin C a day could reduce your risk by 34 per cent. So eat plenty of fresh fruit and vegetables.

## Senior moment

I walked to the Post Office with a letter in one hand and my house keys in the other. While I was there a neighbour stopped to chat. When I got home I realised I still had the letter. I'd posted my keys in the post box! Two hours later the postie emptied the box – he was highly amused.

**Carran Thornton Randall, Middlesex**

## Fast fact

The Greek physician Hippocrates is attributed to be the founder of modern medicine. It was he who recognised the healing powers of salicin – found in the leaves and bark of the willow tree – from which chemist Felix Hoffman later formulated the Aspirin.

## Small talk

I recently had my hair cut in a much shorter style, which I thought looked nice until my six-year-old grandson, Bryan, looked at me in horror saying: "Nan, have you joined the marines?"  **Kay Wallis, Cornwall**

## Fashion we wore

Here's a picture, taken in 1938, of my mother, father and little brother. Dad has his army uniform on and Mum is wearing an oatmeal coloured dress with white calico lace around the collar and a brown belt and shoes. My brother wore a dark blue overcoat and black shoes. Mum said all the clothes were second-hand because we were too poor to afford new.

**Joan Longstone, Foxhill**

## Recipe of the week

### Berried treasures
Serves 4

- 25 g (1 oz) butter
- 1 tbsp golden syrup
- 100 g (4 oz) muesli
- 400 g (16 oz) can of apricots in juice or syrup, chopped and drained
- 400g (16 oz) can of rice pudding
- 400g (16 oz) can of strawberries in juice or syrup, drained
- 400g (16 oz) can of raspberries in juice or syrup, drained

1. In a small saucepan, slowly melt the butter with the golden syrup. Add the muesli, stir to mix and set aside to cool.
2. Divide the apricots evenly between 4 sundae glasses.
3. Cover with 1 tablespoon of rice pudding.
4. Then top with a layer of strawberries followed by a tablespoon of the rice pudding.
5. Then add a layer of the raspberries followed by the rest of the rice pudding.
6. Finally divide the muesli topping evenly between the four glasses and serve immediately.

Recipe: Canned Food UK, www.cannedfood.co.uk

# Lifelong friends

Eileen (2nd row, 5th from the right) and her WAAF pals

In May 1943 I celebrated my 18th birthday and like all girls of that age I had to register to do war work of some kind. I decided to join the WAAF. I'd hardly ever been out of my home village, so the prospect of joining the WAAF was terrifying, especially as I'd have to travel alone. I'd never been on a train and mum came to see me off crying at the station.

When I arrived at Manchester, along with several more recruits, there was RAF transport waiting to take us out to Wilmslow. Dropping our luggage we were marched to the stores and each given two army blankets, two cotton sheets and a pillowslip. Although there was a stove in the middle of the hut, it was so cold very few of us got any sleep that night.

Next morning we were up at six for a wash and brush up before being marched down to the large cookhouse for breakfast. We were kitted out in uniforms and I well remember the grey Air Force bloomers, with elastic in the legs, and the long grey lisle stockings. How I longed for home in that first week – I was terribly homesick but I couldn't ring Mum as we had no telephone. But, as each day wore on, with the companionship of the other girls and lots of laughter, we all began to enjoy ourselves. In the end I made lifelong friends and I wouldn't have missed it for anything.

**Eileen Chapman, North Yorkshire,**

## Plant profile

### Fritillaria uva-vulpis

**Height: 20cm**
**Spread: 15cm**
**Conditions: Thrives in any well-drained soil and light shade.**
Less often seen than its cousins F meleagris and F imperialis, this is one for the enthusiast. Its purple nodding blooms, which are prettily trimmed with yellow, are a delightful sight during spring. Order bulbs during autumn and plant immediately.
Available from specialist suppliers such as www.dejager.co.uk

## Health tip
### Spring clean...
your medicine cabinet. Pills and potions all have use-by dates, so check them out and dispose of anything that isn't in date. Out-of-date medicines can be harmful to your health so return drugs to your chemist to dispose of safely.

## Senior moment
As I went into the kitchen, the light didn't come on straight away and in the semi darkness I saw a shape in front of the microwave. I thought it was my cat as she often sits there. I wanted to use the microwave so I asked her to move. When the light finally came on, I found that I had been gently coaxing a bottle of fabric conditioner!

**Mrs M Evans, Denbighshire**

## Fast fact

Although Heinz Baked Beanz first appeared on shelves in Britain in 1886, it took another 40 years before they were actually made here in the UK. Heinz now makes 1.5 million cans of baked beans every day and only four people ever know the secret recipe at one time.

## Small talk

Our four-year-old grandson was having a riding lesson with two others when after the lesson the instructor asked if anyone had any questions. My grandson put his hand up and asked: "Does Jesus still live in heaven?"

**Jill Revell, Telscombe Cliffs**

## Fashion we wore

**W**hat about this photo, taken by my mum in around 1950? In the picture are me, dad and my brother Gordon. I think it must have been taken on a Sunday because we are all wearing our 'Sunday best'. Although my dad always looked smart, wearing a shirt and tie even to take us for a walk in the afternoon, across the fields to Whittle Hills. I'm wearing a lemon cotton dress with a matching ribbon in my hair and leather sandals. Gordon is wearing short trousers and a white cotton shirt, like dad, but he hated wearing a tie, so that's probably in his pocket!

**Edna Lydiate, Preston**

# Recipe of the week

## Thai coconut chicken soup
### Serves 4

- ◆ 2 lemongrass stalks
- ◆ 1 litre (1³/₄ pint) chicken stock
- ◆ 2 tbsp fresh ginger, coarsely chopped
- ◆ 6 lime leaves (or 2 tbsp coarsely chopped lime zest)
- ◆ 6 shallots, finely sliced
- ◆ 4 chicken thighs, boneless and skinless
- ◆ 3 tbsp fish sauce
- ◆ 4 tbsp lime juice
- ◆ 2 red chillies, deseeded and finely sliced
- ◆ 1 tbsp sugar
- ◆ 1 tbsp red curry paste
- ◆ 1 x 400 g (16 oz) coconut milk
- ◆ 100 g (4 oz) green beans, cut into 2-3 cm lengths
- ◆ 100 g (4 oz) shelled peas
- ◆ Large handful of fresh basil leaves

1. Remove the tough outer layers of the lemon grass and slice into 4 cm (2 in) strips, crushing lightly with the blade of a heavy knife.

2. In a large saucepan, bring the chicken stock to the boil. Add the ginger, lemongrass, lime leaves or zest and half the shallots. Reduce the heat, cover and simmer for an hour.

3. Then strain the stock through a sieve and return to the pan.

4. Cut the chicken pieces into 2.5 cm (1 in) chunks and place in the stock. Add the fish sauce, lime juice, chillies, sugar, red curry paste, coconut milk and the remaining shallots. Bring to the boil, reduce the heat and simmer for 5 minutes.

5. Finally, add the peas and beans and simmer for a further 3-4 minutes, or until the vegetables are just tender and the chicken is cooked.

6. Garnish with the basil leaves and serve immediately.

Recipe: British Beans and Peas, www.tastesofsummer.co.uk

# Biker girls

This photograph was taken in 1948 or 1949, before my husband and I were married. The other ladies and I didn't actually ride the motorbikes – only posed on them for photos! We used to go everywhere on the pillion of the bikes and we all thought we were the bee's knees. The back seats were very small and we used to have to hang on to our boyfriends for dear life in case we fell off.

In those days it was very cheap to go to the coast and we all took our own packed lunch and whatever the weather we ate out – we couldn't afford to have meals in a café. I remember those days very fondly as they were so carefree. I married my boyfriend Len in December 1949 and it will be our 60th wedding

Violet and her friends looking the bee's knees

anniversary this year. Very sadly he won't know it's our anniversary as he is in a nursing home suffering from Alzheimer's. It's my old happy memories that keep me going. In the photograph I'm on the right-hand side. I can't remember the name of the lady in the middle, but the lady on the left was my brother-in-law's ex-girlfriend. He was my husband's twin and died in 2005. Those days were such fun.

**Violet Dunkling, Swindon**

## Plant profile

### Trillium sessile

**Height: 30cm**
**Spread: 30cm**
**Conditions: Enjoys moist well-drained soil in partial shade. Add plenty of organic matter when planting.**
Woodland gardens are a haven on sunny days and few shade-lovers are as spectacular as trilliums. With three large beautifully mottled leaves, trilliums create real impact, especially when their deep red flowers appear during the spring. Available from specialist bulb suppliers such as www.dejager.co.uk

## Health tip
### Stick on your sunnies

Make sure you wear your sunglasses on bright days. They'll help to protect your eyes from ageing UV damage. If you need a new pair ensure they have a label that say they have UV filters.

## Senior moment

It cost quite a bit to have our poorly cat put to sleep. While we were out I saw a soft toy cat in a shop window for £12. I said to my husband that it would've been cheaper to have Molly stuffed. He replied: "Well she'd have to be dead first." I didn't think about that!

**Mrs Wilkinson, Lincolnshire**

## Fast fact

Everyone's favourite pizza the Margherita was named after Queen Margherita Teresa Giovanni, the consort of Umberto. The classic pizza was made especially in honour of her visit to Naples in 1889. It used ingredients to reflect the colours of the Italian flag with tomatoes, mozzarella cheese and basil – delicious!

## Small talk

My grandson had heard his parents discussing that I was to have an eye test. To which he remarked: "I need one too, I can't see a thing when I'm in bed and you put the light out."

**Mrs E Jones, Ruthin**

## Fashion we wore

**H**ere's an interesting photo, taken in 1952. My eldest brother, Peter, was getting married in Dewsbury – about 11 miles from where we lived. None of our friends or family could afford a car and taxis were out of the question. Luckily, my Uncle Harry was a part-time driver for a local coach company and arranged to borrow a vehicle to drive everyone to the church. I'm not in the picture because I was a bridesmaid, so had gone to church with the bride. But we all came back on the coach, singing along to old community songs. My grandma had died earlier that year and my mum and her sisters had bought clothes for the funeral. Obviously they couldn't afford new outfits so they ended up dressed rather sombrely for the wedding

**Janet Cooper, Huddersfield**

# Recipe of the week

## Passion cake
### Serves 12

- ◆ 150 g (6 oz) plain flour
- ◆ 1 tsp bicarbonate of soda
- ◆ 1 tsp baking powder
- ◆ 1 tsp ground cinnamon
- ◆ Pinch of salt
- ◆ 225 g (9 oz) carrots, peeled and coarsely grated
- ◆ 75 g (3 oz) walnuts, chopped
- ◆ 3 large Lion Quality eggs
- ◆ 175ml (7 fl oz) sunflower oil
- ◆ 150 g (6 oz) caster sugar
- ◆ 2 tsp vanilla essence

For the topping:
- ◆ 150 g (6 oz) full fat soft cheese
- ◆ 25 g (1 oz) icing sugar, sifted
- ◆ $1/2$ tsp vanilla essence
- ◆ 12 walnut halves
Ribbon, to decorate (optional)

1. Preheat the oven to 170°C/325°F/Gas Mark 3. Oil and base line two 20 cm (8 in) round cake tins.
2. In a large mixing bowl, sift the first five ingredients. Add the carrots and walnuts.
3. In a separate bowl, beat the eggs, oil, sugar and vanilla together, add this to the mixing bowl and beat until combined.
4. Divide between two cake tins, then bake in the centre of the oven for 1 hour, or until the cakes are cooked through. Cool in the tins for 5 minutes, before leaving to cool on a wire rack.
5. For the topping: Beat the cream cheese, icing sugar and vanilla essence in a bowl until smooth. Place half the icing on top of one cake and put the other cake on top. Spread the remainder of the icing on top of the cakes and decorate with walnut halves. Tie a ribbon around for decoration if required.

Recipe: British Lion Eggs, www.eggrecipes.co.uk

# I remember Green Shield stamps

BY: MARION CLARKE

It took a lot of time – and a lot of lick – to fill your book with Green Shield stamps but in the Sixties and Seventies we were all busily licking and sticking to save for desirable consumer goods such as a Kenwood Chef (33¼ books) a Regentone TV set (88 books) or a Silver Cloud motor boat (a mere 170 books).

Yes, you could buy almost anything with Green Shield stamps and you got them everywhere – they were handed out with purchases at your local butchers, greengrocers, chemist and petrol stations. Even supermarkets like Tesco got in on the act, although other

GREEN SHIELD
STAMP SAVER BOOK
FOR BOTH REGULAR
AND THE NEW BIG 10 STAMP

PIC: REX FEATURES

around – competitors included Pink Stamps, Blue Star and Yellow Stamps – but the Green Shield Trading Stamp Company was the first

motor boat you would need a staggering 217,600 stamps and would have had to spend £5,440, roughly the equivalent of what you would have paid for a large detached house!

Not surprisingly, most of us set our sights on something more modest, like the Kenwood Chef, for which we'd have had to fork out a more realistic £1,064 on groceries and petrol.

Green Shield stamps were so much part of our lives they even got a mention in a pop song when Genesis punned 'Knights of the Green Shield stamp and shout' on their album Selling

England by the Pound. And an American guest at Fawlty Towers asked: "What do you get for living in a climate like this? Green Stamps?"

By the end of the 1970s the stamps' popularity had waned as it dawned on customers that they were ultimately paying for the gifts in the price of the goods bought. Or maybe we just found better things to do with our time than sticking hundreds of little stamps into books.

In 1973 the Green Shield catalogue shops were rebranded Argos which finally ceased selling stamps in 1991.

## What do you get for living in a climate like this? Green Shield stamps?

major retailers such as Sainsbury's, Marks and Spencer, Boots and W H Smith refrained. In fact, Lord Sainsbury opposed trading stamps and his opposition led to an Act of Parliament to regulate the stamp companies.

Green Shield weren't the only stamps

on the scene, launched in 1958 by entrepreneur Richard Tompkins who brought the concept over from America.

This is how they worked. You got one stamp for each sixpence spent and each book contained 1,280 stamps. To get the Silver Cloud

# Quiz of the month

All these events took place in the month of April over the past 60 years, but can you arrange them in the order that they happened?

PIC: REX FEATURES

**F** The American black civil rights leader, Dr Martin Luther King, has been shot dead in the southern US city of Memphis, Tennessee.

**G** The Soviet Union has acknowledged there has been an accident at the Chernobyl nuclear power plant in Ukraine.

**H** There have been scenes of jubilation in Baghdad as US tanks rolled into the very heart of the Iraqi capital, confirming that the government of Saddam Hussein has been ousted from power.

**I** Red Rum has galloped into racing history by winning the Grand National for a record third time.

**J** Prince Rainier III of Monaco has married the American film actress Grace Kelly.

**K** President Richard Nixon has taken full responsibility for the Watergate scandal but has denied any personal involvement.

**L** Neil Kinnock has resigned as Labour leader following the party's defeat by the Conservatives in the general election .

**M** At least 93 football supporters have been crushed to death at Hillsborough Stadium, in Britain's worst-ever sporting disaster.

**N** Argentina has invaded the British territory of the Falkland Islands in the south Atlantic.

**O** WPC Yvonne Fletcher has been killed and ten people injured after shots were fired from the Libyan embassy in central London.

**P** A huge car bomb has exploded at a US Government building in Oklahoma City, killing at least 80 people including 17 children at a nursery

News stories taken from http://news.bbc.co.uk/onthisday/

**A** Thousands of well-wishers greeted the Queen and the Duke of Edinburgh when they arrived at Clydeside to launch the new royal yacht, Britannia.

**B** The world number one women's tennis player, Monica Seles, has been stabbed in the back during a quarter-final match in Hamburg.

**C** The moving diary of Anne Frank, a Jewish victim of the Holocaust, is now available in British bookshops entitled The Diary of a Young Girl.

**D** The BBC has received a mixed reaction to a spoof Panorama programme about spaghetti crops in Switzerland, broadcast on April Fool's Day.

**E** NASA has successfully launched the space shuttle Discovery on its historic mission to carry the Hubble space telescope into orbit above the Earth.

Answer: C) 1952, A) 1953, J) 1956, D) 1957, F) 1968, K) 1973, I) 1977, N) 1982, O) 1984, G) 1986, M) 1989, E) 1990, L) 1992, B) 1993, P) 1995, H) 2003.

# The bells, the bells!

BY: SUSAN SARAPUK

## Bells and goldfish are the bane of Mrs Barley's life

"**A**lastair Flynn! What do you think you're doing?" The boy looked up from the pond in Mrs Barley's garden, a picture of innocence. He held a bag in which six goldfish were swimming.

"I'm releasing them," he said, implying it should have been obvious.

"Into my pond?"

"I won them at the fair. It's not right, keeping them in plastic bags – Miss Penhaligon said."

"It's not right to trespass on other people's property, either."

"Sorry."

"Silly boy! You can't save every goldfish in the world."

"I've saved these ones, though."

## "You can't save every goldfish in the world."

She watched him scamper away. He didn't seem to be afraid of her like the other children.

Then the bells began to ring. Those infernal church bells! It really was too bad when a person couldn't have peace in her own home. She put in earplugs and began to scrub the sink.

After practice, the ringers went to the pub. Rosemary Penhaligon loved the camaraderie even if some people thought bell ringing was slightly eccentric.

"That tenor's sounding swell now, Clive," said Hilary Beamish. "It's a pity we can't practise more," Clive growled. "Especially with the competition coming up. If it wasn't for that interfering old…" He took a gulp of beer.

"She's the only one who objects," Roger Hellston sighed. "And it isn't as if she is one of those incomers who like the countryside to be deadly silent."

"Somebody should shoot her," Clive suggested among chuckles.

On Sunday Rosemary Penhaligon passed Barley Mow House.

"So you're the one putting silly ideas into children's heads!"

Mrs Barley scowled at her over the hedge.

"What's this nonsense you're teaching Alastair Flynn? Him and his goldfish."

"Well, Alastair's a bright boy. If he decided to save a few goldfish it would have been his own idea."

"Tsk!" Mrs Barley turned away.

Rosemary couldn't help smiling to herself as she entered the bell tower where a babble of voices greeted her.

"It's Clive!" said Hilary explained. "He's broken his arm, fell off his mower."

"Poor Clive," Rosemary sympathised.

"Poor Clive? Poor us! Where will we get a replacement before the competition?"

The next day there was a knock at Mrs Barley's door. She clicked her tongue impatiently as she went to answer it.

"What do you want, Alastair Flynn?"

"I came to say thank you for looking after the fish."

"I'm not looking after them! For all I know, the cat has had them!"

"I've brought some food." He held up a packet.

"I haven't got time to be feeding fish."

"I'll do it, if you like," he said disappearing around the side of the house.

**S**he watched him from the kitchen window. The sight of his slight form bending down in the long summer grass took her breath away. Then he turned and waved to her. Mrs Barley went to the back door. "Go home now!" she shouted.

There were no bells on Tuesday evening. When she saw the schoolteacher in the shop, Mrs Barley said: "So you've finally decided to listen to me."

Rosemary turned around. "Oh, you mean the bells. One of our ringers has broken his arm so we can't enter the competition."

"At last we'll have a bit of peace!" Mrs Barley sniffed, trying to ignore the look of pity on the younger woman's face. She didn't want pity.

One morning she found herself bending over the pond watching the fish in its grey depths and thinking how they must be enjoying their freedom. She straightened up. Fish were fish, for goodness' sake! Fish didn't have feelings.

PIC: KATE DAVIES

# Maybe he saved crabby old women, too

She stomped back up the path, to find Alastair standing at the back door.

"Have you been visiting the fish?"

"Fish don't need visiting, you silly boy. What are you doing here? Haven't you got anything better to do?"

"Will you sponsor me?" he held up a piece of paper and a pen. "We're raising money to help the donkey sanctuary."

"Tsk!" she said, scribbling on the paper.

"Can I come and see the fish again tomorrow?" he asked.

"If you must."

The next day she gave him some milk and a biscuit. "Do you have any children?" he asked.

"No!" she snapped, then added: "I used to have a little boy. His name was Thomas."

"What happened?" Alastair observed her over the rim of his glass.

"He died when he was small."

"Is that why you don't go out and people think you're nasty?"

She was about to protest but said instead: "When Thomas died I didn't want to enjoy myself any more."

"That's sad. I'm going to see the fish now." He slid off the chair and dashed outside.

Why did this child bother with her, she wondered? He'd saved the fish – maybe he saved crabby old women, too.

In the church, the ringers were assembled.

Roger said: "I asked my brother to ring but he doesn't live in the village so it would be against the rules."

"We can't enter the competition, let's just forget it."

They went to their places. Roger was about to start calling when the door clicked and Mrs Barley entered.

"Now what?" Hilary demanded.

Mrs Barley cleared her throat. "I heard you're a ringer short."

"What's that to you?" Roger exploded but Rosemary placed a restraining hand on his arm.

"I used to be a ringer," Mrs Barley continued. "A long time ago…"

They stared at her, open-mouthed. "So, if I can make a difference…"

Rosemary hugged her: "All the difference in the world, Mrs Barley."

# May 2010

Saturday

1

Sunday

2

Monday

3
      **May Day (Bank Holiday)**

Tuesday

4

Wednesday

5

Thursday

6

Friday

7

Saturday

8

Sunday

9

Monday

10

Tuesday

11

Wednesday

12

Thursday

13

Friday

14

Saturday

15

Sunday

16

Monday

17

Tuesday

18

Wednesday

19

Thursday

20

Friday

21

Saturday

22

| | |
|---|---|
| Sunday **23** | Friday **28** |
| Pentecost (Whit Sunday) | |
| Monday **24** | Saturday **29** |
| Tuesday **25** | Sunday **30** |
| Wednesday **26** | Monday **31** |
| | Spring Bank Holiday |
| Thursday **27** | |

PIC: REX FEATURES

## Poetry corner

## Silver surfer

The computer swallowed Nana,
Honestly it's true.
She pressed Control and Enter,
And disappeared from view.

It devoured her completely,
The thought just made me squirm.
She might have caught a virus,
Or been eaten by a worm.

I've searched through the recycle bin,
And files of every kind.
I've even used the Internet,
But nothing I could find.

In desperation I asked Jeeves,
My searchers to refine.
The reply came back negative,
Not a thing was found online.

So if inside your inbox,
My Nana you should see.
Please copy, scan and paste her,
And send her back to me.

**Mrs Maureen Tunstall, Preston**

# My secret love

**N**o sooner does the back door shut behind my husband than I sneak off to my favourite place. I settle myself on my piano stool and the pristine ivory keys seem to smile a welcome. I even practise in the middle of the night when my husband is asleep. This isn't because he's unkind, but because he hates the sound of a piano – especially one played badly.

I've wanted to play the piano for as long as I can remember. Brought up in a family where the piano played central role in our evening's entertainment, I longed to be able to have lessons. Sadly, it wasn't to be, so I learnt to play by ear and enjoyed tinkering for hours on end.

Now at the grand age of 66 my dream has

Mary with her long-awaited piano

come true and I've used a small legacy to buy my own piano and stool. I chose a basic piano even though I knew it would be difficult to master with arthritic fingers, forgetfulness and a diminishing concentration span. My fingers aren't as nimble as they used to be and my hand-and-eye-coordination isn't great. I know I'll never be a concert pianist, play Carmen with Pomposo or as an opera buff travel to Verona. But I enjoy it in my own small way and might even reach grade three standard or play a piece of music stretching over a number of pages. Who knows what dizzy heights await me and my secret love.

**Mary Jones, Mid Glamorgan**

---

## Plant profile

### Erythronium 'Pagoda'

**Height: 50cm**
**Spread: 15cm**
**Conditions: Thrives in moist soil and partial shade.**
This graceful spring–flowering bulb begs closer inspection and never disappoints. With pretty reflexed blooms and elegantly arching stems, it has a subtle beauty that makes it a popular choice. Spreading by offsets, it quickly produces an impressive clump and when it has, is best left completely undisturbed. Widely available from garden centres, it has an Award of Garden Merit from the RHS.

---

## Health tip

### Treat your feet...

to a trip to a podiatrist before sandal season arrives. They'll ensure that your toes are in top health before you have to get them out for the world. Visit www.feetforlife.org to find one in your area.

---

## Senior moment

Going out, I left my partner in the house to let in the man who was servicing the boiler. When I got home I found that I'd locked the door behind me and taken the keys! The boiler man had to climb in through a window and remarked that he'd heard of wives locking husbands out, but never in before!

**Barbara Neal, Pembrokeshire**

## Fast fact

It's the beginning of hayfever season but did you know that during the 6th Century it was customary to congratulate people who sneezed because it was thought that they were expelling evil from their bodies? During the great plague Pope Gregory I ordered everyone to say, 'God bless you' to anyone who sneezed.

## Small talk

My grandson, aged three, was asking me about the security doors in a children's soft play area. I carefully explained that if anyone tried to break in at night an alarm would sound and a light would flash. He asked where the light was and I pointed to the nearest I could see. He looked doubtful and said: "I don't think so Nana, but good try."  **Valerie Humphries, Swindon**

## Fashion we wore

I thought readers would like to see this photo of me. When I was in my teens I belonged to a club in our village called the Girls Friendly Society. Every year we had a May Day celebration, with country dancing and a Maypole. In 1959 it was my turn to be the 'May Queen'. In the photo Mrs Hearn, the wife of the comedian Mr Pastry, is crowning me with a garland of flowers.

**Vivienne Collins, Tonbridge**

# Recipe of the week

## Smoked ham and asparagus tart
**Serves 4**

◆ 500 g (20 oz) short crust pastry
◆ 6 large eggs
◆ 300 ml (12 fl oz) double cream
◆ 100 g (4 oz) Parmesan cheese, grated
◆ Salt and pepper
◆ 2 bundles of British asparagus, trimmed
◆ 150 g (6 oz) smoked ham

1. Preheat the oven to 180°C/350°F/Gas Mark 4. Line a 23 cm (9 inch) tart case. Roll out the pastry and put into the tart case. Prick the base of the pastry and chill for 30 minutes.
2. Place parchment paper on top of the pastry and add baking beans, then bake in the oven for 15 minutes, or until the pastry starts to firm up. Remove from the oven and leave to cool slightly.
3. In a mixing bowl, beat the eggs, cream and Parmesan together and season.
4. Scatter the asparagus and ham over the pastry case and pour on the egg mixture.
5. Place the tart in the middle of the oven for 25 minutes, or until set.
6. Serve warm or cold with a fresh salad.

Recipe: British Asparagus, www.british–asparagus.co.uk

# Dreaming of Margate

Growing up in the 1920s, many children never got to see the sea. I was one of the fortunate ones because my father asserted that a holiday was a good investment and prevented visits to the doctor in the winter months. We lived in Southall, Middlesex at the time and we always went to Margate in Kent. As a young child that one glorious week during the school holidays, was like going to paradise. The excitement started on embarkation on the Royal Sovereign, a paddle steamer, which transported holidaymakers from London Bridge to Margate Pier. We'd sit on slatted benches eating fish paste sandwiches willing the miles away, eager to get to our destination. My uncle, who was six years my senior, always came with us and we stayed with the same landlady, Mrs Epps, each year.

Madeleine practising her acrobatic routine.

The Concert Party on the beach held talent competitions three times a week and I would enter doing a ballet, tap or acrobatic dance routine in rotation. Then Mrs Epps would keep an eye on us in the evenings while my parents went for a walk. Us kids would gaze excitedly out of the back bedroom window and watch Dreamland Amusement Park. Margate has such golden memories and everything seemed magical then. One whiff of frying bacon in the early morning wafts me back and I am once again that small child walking with my Dad past the posh hotels. Little did I dream then, that one day I would be living not many miles from the town of my dreams.

**Madeleine Croll, Whitstable**

## Plant profile

### Arisaema sikokianum

**Height: 50cm**
**Spread: 15cm**
**Conditions: Thrives in moist, well-drained soils, preferably neutral or acidic, and heavy shade.**

Spectacular in appearance, this strange-looking plant will be a real talking point in your garden. Its large-lobed leaves are a perfect backdrop for the enormous purple spathe (hood-like bract) and white spadix (flower) it produces during the spring. A great woodland plant, it's available from specialist bulb suppliers such as www.dejager.co.uk. (Take care as the sap may irritate.)

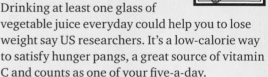

## Health tip
### Weight loss secret

Drinking at least one glass of vegetable juice everyday could help you to lose weight say US researchers. It's a low-calorie way to satisfy hunger pangs, a great source of vitamin C and counts as one of your five-a-day.

## Senior moment

Sinking gratefully into my seat on the bus, I was feeling very pleased with my morning of shopping. Until halfway home and it suddenly dawned on me that I had come in my car!

**Maureen Jones, Merseyside**

## Fast fact

On May 6, 1840 the world's first adhesive postage stamp the Penny Black became valid for UK use. More than 68 million Penny Black stamps were issued,which meant, that at last, sending items through the post became affordable for all.

## Small talk

Asking my son what he wanted for breakfast he replied: "Mummy, I'll have eggs on toast – but without the eggs."

**Iris Ann Dutton, West Midlands**

## Fashion we wore

During the war, the ship that I was on was sailing near the coast of Malaysia when we stopped for a spot of shore leave. The first thing we came across was a market and I spotted some lovely dress material, a sky blue one and a pale lemon one. I bought a length of each and sent it home to my wife, Joyce.

When I arrived home some time later I found Joyce had got the material made into dresses. The one in the photograph is the lemon one, with a brown trim – lovely isn't it?

**Edward Carey, Kingston-upon-Hull**

# Recipe of the week

PIC: STEVE BAXTER

## Little banoffee pies
### Serves 6

- ◆ 250 g (8 oz) digestive biscuits
- ◆ 100 g (4 oz) butter, melted
- ◆ 400 g can (16 oz) Carnation Caramel
- ◆ 3 small ripe bananas
- ◆ 284 ml (7 oz) carton whipping cream, softly whipped
- ◆ Cocoa powder, to decorate

1. To make the base, blitz the biscuits in a food processor, until they resemble fine crumbs and then combine with the melted butter.
2. Either grease 6 individual 9 cm (3.5 inch) loose-bottomed flan tins or a deep 18 cm (7 inch) loose-bottomed cake tin.
3. Using the back of a teaspoon, press the mixture into the base and sides of the tin(s). Chill for about 20 minutes.
4. Divide the caramel between the bases. Remove the pies from the tins.
5. Slice the bananas, reserving six slices for decoration, fold the rest into the softly whipped cream.
6. Spoon over the caramel and decorate each pie with a banana slice and dust with cocoa.

◆ **Top tip:** This recipe makes a tasty sundae. Layer the crushed biscuits (without the melted butter) and other ingredients into sundae glasses and chill until ready to serve.

Recipe: Nestlé Carnation, www.carnation.co.uk

# My allotment

**M**y love of gardening started way back when my parents gave me a small plot of my own to grow things in. I can't remember if I actually succeeded in getting anything to grow but it started my great love for growing flowers and vegetables. When I retired the idea of getting an allotment appealed to me as it would free up my garden for more flowers instead of half of it being used to grow vegetables.

My husband agreed to help me, so our name was added to the council allotment waiting list. Nine months later we heard that a plot was free on the site we wanted. In April 2008 we took over plot nine. It wasn't in a bad state – some have weeds

Trish's ordered allotment is hard work but lots of fun.

waist high – ours was manageable.

It took us about a month to get it weeded and ready for planting. I'd already planted seeds in my greenhouse in the hope we'd have somewhere to put them. We had a plan for the planting, but that didn't last very long as our enthusiasm took over. We wanted everything, so in went onions, beetroot, carrots, peas, celeriac and potatoes. For beginners we had a very good harvest, especially strawberries – I even made jam. Now in our second year the eagerness is still with us. We cross our fingers for another good harvest come the autumn, it's a lot of hard work, but it's also a lot of fun.

**Trish Wapling, Uxbridge, Middlesex**

## Plant profile

### Aquilegia vulgaris

**Height: 50cm**
**Spread: 35cm**
**Conditions: Thrives in moist soil and enjoys the dappled sunlight of a cottage garden border.**
Commonly called columbines or granny's bonnets, aquilegias produce flowers in almost every colour of the rainbow. They flower in late spring and summer and will self-seed throughout the garden. Rather promiscuous in habit, you can never predict what the offspring will be like, and may well generate a great new garden-worthy variety. Widely available from garden centres.

## Health tip
### Seek out the sun

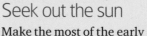

Make the most of the early summer sunshine – it's a great way to top-up your levels of immune-boosting vitamin D. Scientists at the University of Warwick have found that 92 per cent of 50-70 year olds don't have enough vitamin D.

## Senior moment

I went into a posh jewellery shop and asked the assistant to put a new battery in my watch as it had stopped. She looked at me and rather pityingly said: "Madam, you've got the winder pulled out, that's why it has stopped." **Mrs Minister, Suffolk**

## Fast fact

The longest ever screen kiss was between Regis Toomey and Jane Wyman in the 1941 hit comedy You're in the Army Now. The pair smooched for an impressive three minutes and five seconds – she was married to future US president Ronald Reagan at the time.

## Small talk

My uncle was helping a distressed lady and her young daughter look for her son who had gone missing on the beach. After a while, the young girl turned to her mother and said: "If he doesn't come back can I have his bedroom?"

**C F Banks, Hampshire**

## Fashion we wore

This photograph shows my mother, aged 20, resplendent in an outfit she wore for a friend's wedding in 1955. All her accessories were white and the dress various shades of green. The hat had white feathers, which were fashionable at the time. The shoes she's wearing are actually the shoes she had bought for her own wedding but she had decided to 'wear them in' before her own big day. My late father took the photo and he thought she looked the bee's knees!

**Janet Griffiths,
Lichfield, Staffs**

## Recipe of the week

### Light roasted mushroom and onion tartlets

**Makes 4**

- ◆ 4 sheets filo pastry
- ◆ 1 large egg white, lightly beaten
- ◆ 3 medium red onions, each cut into 12 wedges
- ◆ 1 tbsp olive oil
- ◆ 4 tbsp red pesto
- ◆ 250 g (10 oz) oyster mushrooms, sliced
- ◆ Juice of one lime
- ◆ Salt and pepper

1. Pre-heat the oven to 200° C/400°F/Gas Mark 6.
2. Lay one sheet of filo pastry on the work surface and brush with egg white. Fold in half, then brush top with more egg white. Fold in half again to give a 20 x 15 cm (8 inch x 6 inch) rectangles.
3. Use these filo pastry sheets to line the base and sides of a 10 cm (4 inch) round loose-bottomed fluted flan tin, pressing the pastry into flutes, trimming any excess.
4. Line three more flan tins with the remaining filo pastry. Bake for 8 minutes.
5. Remove from the flan tins, carefully brush outside with egg white, and then place upside down on a baking sheet.
6. Put the onion wedges in a roasting tin and drizzle over the oil. Roast for 10-15 minutes.
7. Stir in the red pesto and mushrooms and roast for a further 8-10 minutes. Returning the flan cases to the oven for the final 5 minutes of this.
8. Spoon the roasted onion mixture into the warm filo pastry cases and drizzle with lime juice. Serve immediately with a fresh salad.

Recipe: Mushroom Bureau, www.mushroom–uk.com

# That September

I have vivid memories of being evacuated on September 1, 1939. I attended Vernon Square School, Kings Cross, which was a very large school. During that summer we attended school, not to have lessons, but to play and be drilled. On August 31, we were told we would be evacuated the next day. When the school gates opened that day the road outside was mobbed with mums. I think it's unlikely that anyone found their own children, but they took any child's case and carried it for them.

We walked to the station, which on arrival was chaotic as families weren't allowed in. The train journey seemed to last forever, but I have a wonderful memory of the train stopping at a station

Kitty at the seaside with her mother, aunt and brother

and porters lining up on the platform passing thick white china cups of water through the windows to us. I still get teary-eyed when I remember their concern. I was taken, with three other girls, to a place called St Marks. I was very lucky as I was billeted in the local manor house owned by a Mr Tinsley who was a very big landowner in Lincolnshire and he only used the house once every month or so. The residents of the house were the cook and housekeeper, her husband the gardener and their daughter. Mrs Wool was a fabulous cook and I'll never forget her homemade Victoria plum jam and she made the lightest of puddings.

**Kitty Fuller, Barnet**

## Plant profile

### Nemesia denticulata 'Confetti'

**Height: 30cm**
**Spread: 60cm**
**Conditions: Enjoys well-drained soil in sun or shade.**
A hardy perennial, this variety has proved extremely popular with gardeners, producing scented, sugar–pink flowers and a mound of pretty leaves. It flowers reliably all summer long and looks great in brightly–coloured containers or planted in swathes across a border. Use it to fill any last minute gaps. Available online at www.hayloft-plants.co.uk

## Health tip
### It's Strawberry season...

so make the most of them.
They're packed with anti-ageing vitamin C and antioxidant flavonoids, which could help to fight off wrinkles and keep you in good health. Serve them with fat-free Greek yoghurt if you're watching your waistline.

## Senior moment

I recently stayed with my mother-in-law, Barbara, for a family occasion. Opening the door to some guests unknown to me, I introduced myself as 'Daughter's Barbara-in-law!'  **Mrs C Riley, Essex**

# Fast fact

The onion was the favourite vegetable of the Ancient Egyptians, who saw its round shape and concentric rings as a symbol of eternal life. When Rameses IV died in 1160 BC he even had onions put into his eye sockets!

# Small talk

My friend was visiting with her five-year-old son, Sebastian. Finding a pair of earphones he pretended to be a doctor with a stethoscope. Joining in I dramatically lay on the sofa and I said: "I was watching TV when I fainted, what's wrong with me doctor?" He thought for a moment and replied: "I think you've got square eyes from watching too much television!"

**Helen Connett, Bournemouth**

# Fashion we wore

I thought readers might like to see this photo, taken in Bournemouth in 1937, of me and my sister Margaret. I was just 16 year old and on my first trip to England from Ireland, to stay with my big sister. I'm on the right, wearing a blue coat and blue and white dress. My mammy made the dress especially for the trip.

**Nancy Hendley, Liverpool**

# Recipe of the week

## Carrot cake muffins
**Makes 10-12**

- ◆ 225 g (9 oz) butter, softened
- ◆ 225 g (9 oz) soft light brown sugar
- ◆ 3 medium eggs, separated
- ◆ Finely grated zest of 1 orange
- ◆ 2 tsp lemon juice
- ◆ 180 g (7 oz) self-raising flour
- ◆ 1 tsp baking powder
- ◆ 75 g (3 oz) ground almonds
- ◆ 125 g (5 oz) walnuts, roughly chopped
- ◆ 175 g (7 oz) carrots, peeled and grated

For the topping:
- ◆ 225g (9 oz) cream cheese
- ◆ 2 tsp runny honey

1. Preheat the oven to 180°C/350°F/Gas Mark 4. Line a muffin tin with paper cases.
2. In a large mixing bowl, cream together the butter and sugar until pale. Add the egg yolks one at a time, beating well in-between.
3. Sift in the flour before adding the zest and baking powder. Fold in the lemon juice, ground almonds, walnuts and carrots.
4. In a separate bowl whisk the egg whites until they form soft peaks. Fold gently but thoroughly into the cake mixture. Spoon into the muffin cases, leaving a slight hollow in the centre of each one.
5. Bake for 10–15 minutes, or until risen and golden. Leave to completely cool on a wire rack.
6. For the topping, beat together the cream cheese and honey until smooth, and spread over the muffin tops.

Recipe: British Carrots, www.britishcarrots.co.uk

# I remember I'm backing Britain

## BY: MARION CLARKE

For a few months in the winter of 1967/68, the whole country was caught up in the heady excitement of the I'm Backing Britain campaign. It all started at Colt, a company in Surbiton that manufactured air conditioning equipment. Inspired by a memo from the managing director, five of the secretaries volunteered to work an extra half hour each day to boost productivity.

The pound had just been devalued and British exports were suffering so the move was naturally welcomed by the Prime Minster, Harold Wilson. The press was enthusiastic, too. The Daily Express ran a picture of the secretaries with the headline 'The Girls Britain Can Be Proud Of' and even the Financial Times described the move as 'a beacon of light in an otherwise dismal economic and industrial prospect'.

Within a week, the campaign

The I'm Backing Britain campaign attracted supporters from all walks of life.

## Within a week the campaign had spread

had spread nationwide. Thousands followed Colt's lead in various ways; some companies cancelled projected price increases while others waived fees. One betting shop got into the spirit of things by opening its doors half an hour earlier every day. Union Jack flags appeared in every high street and the

Royal Mail produced an 'I'm Backing Britain' franking mark.

Many well-known names were keen to do their bit. The Duke of Edinburgh sent a telegram to say this was the most heartening news he'd heard in 1967. Herman's Hermits agreed to donate the royalties from their next record. The poet laureate wrote a special poem. Most famously, Tony Hatch and Jackie Trent composed a song for Bruce Forsyth with the lyrics:

**I'm backing Britain
Yes, I'm backing Britain
We're all backing Britain.
The feeling is growing
So let's keep it going
The good times
are blowing away.**
Everyone involved in making

the record took cuts in their fees so that it could be priced at 5s instead of the usual 7s 4d for a single.

But, sadly, Bruce's patriotic ditty didn't make the charts and the campaign also began to ran out of steam. Things were made worse when it was revealed that the 'I'm Backing Britain' T-shirts had actually been made in Portugal because it hadn't been possible to find a British company that could give the same quality for the price.

Beatle Paul McCartney dismissed the whole campaign as ridiculous and wrote a satirical song called I'm Backing the UK which eventually became better known as Back in the USSR.

# Quiz of the month

All these events took place in the month of May over the past 60 years, but can you arrange them in the order that they happened?

PIC: REX FEATURES

**A** Britain's first astronaut, 27-year-old Helen Sharman from Sheffield, blasted into orbit.

**B** Britain's first heart transplant is successfully carried out at the National Heart Hospital in Marylebone, London.

**C** Graeme Hick, Worcestershire's 21-year-old prodigy, has scored more than 400 runs in a county championship match – the highest innings in England this century.

**D** Hunger striker Bobby Sands has died in prison 66 days after first refusing to eat. The 27-year-old republican spent the last days of his life on a water bed to protect his fragile bones.

**E** Ian Brady and his lover Myra Hindley are sentenced to life imprisonment for the 'Moors murders'.

**F** King George VI has inaugurated the Festival of Britain and opened the Royal Festival Hall on London's South Bank.

**G** Long queues have appeared at garages and motorists have torn their ration books into confetti after the government announced an end to petrol rationing.

**H** Nelson Mandela has become South Africa's first black president after more than three centuries of white rule. Mr Mandela's African National Congress (ANC) party won 252 of the 400 seats in the first democratic elections in South Africa's history.

**I** Princess Margaret and Anthony Armstrong Jones have married at Westminster Abbey. More than 20 million viewers tuned in to watch the first ever televised royal wedding service.

**J** Roger Bannister, a 25-year-old British medical student, has become the first man to run a mile in less than four minutes.

**K** Sir Francis Chichester has arrived home in his yacht, Gypsy Moth IV, having completed his epic single-handed voyage around the world.

**L** The Daily Sketch newspaper, which was founded in 1909, has been published for the last time.

**M** The Labour Party has won the general election in a landslide victory, leaving the Conservatives in tatters after 18 years in power. Tony Blair promised he would deliver 'unity and purpose for the future'.

**N** The New Zealander, Edmund Hillary, and the Nepalese Sherpa Tenzing Norgay, have become the first people to reach the summit of Mount Everest on the Nepal-Tibet border.

**O** The official wing of the IRA in Northern Ireland has announced a ceasefire, while reserving the right of self-defence against attacks by the British Army and sectarian groups.

**P** Twelve weeks before the opening ceremony of the Los Angeles Olympic Games, the USSR has announced it is boycotting them. It is expected most of the Eastern Bloc will follow suit.

News stories taken from http://news.bbc.co.uk/onthisday/

ANSWER: G) 1950, F) 1951, N) 1953, J) 1954, I) 1960, E) 1966, K) 1967, B) 1968, L) 1971, O) 1972, D) 1981, P) 1984, C) 1988, A) 1991, H) 1994, M) 1997

# All at sea

BY: MARY WINDSOR

## Jane's dream holiday is very different from her friend Rita's

Jane examined her face in the mirror. Her 60 years were beginning to show. The wrinkles were winning! Her reflection in the mirror showed green eyes with a hint of mischief. She thought, 'Might as well be cheerful as I can't afford a facelift'.

She grabbed her handbag and keys, slammed the front door and almost tripped over the large marmalade cat sprawled on the doormat.

"Ginger!" she reproached him.

"He's enjoying the sun. Not in a rush, like his owner!"

Jane turned to see the postman, Jim.

"He'll still be there when I get back," she said as he handed over her mail. "Expecting his tea!"

## Rita's wrinkles were well under control

"Did you hear that, fella?" Jim tickled the cat's ears. "The young lady says you'll be waiting when she returns!"

"Thanks for the 'young'," Jane laughed, "got to dash, I'm meeting a friend for coffee."

"Not George Clooney?" he teased.

"I wish!" she grinned. "No, it's a girlfriend who won't like to be kept waiting."

Jim watched as she hurried away. Shrugging the mailbag onto his shoulder. This was the last street on his round and his own house was in the next road.

Jane got off the bus in the town centre.

"You're late!"

"The bus was late, Rita. I wasn't!" Jane defended herself.

"Let's go straight to Carlo's and I can tell you about my cruise!" Rita gushed, patting her new hairdo as they crossed the road.

"It's very different to your usual style," Jane offered cautiously, thinking it was too short and too blonde for an older person. Even one as well preserved as Rita. Rita's wrinkles were well under control! She had recently visited an expensive cosmetic clinic to 'have some work done'.

They found a corner table and sipped their lattes. Rita was eager to impress Jane with details of the cruise.

"Debs says it's an ideal holiday to meet a man! It's so romantic at sea!" Meeting a (preferably wealthy) man was Rita's prime aim in life.

"And pricey!" Jane replied, reading the glossy brochure Rita produced from her handbag.

They ran through the itinerary suggested by Rita's daughter, Debs. Jane wasn't keen on Debs. She encouraged her mother's natural extravagance.

Fortunately, Rita was comfortably off. Jane's civil service pension was a generous one and she could have accompanied Rita but a cruise wasn't her style. She liked a restful holiday with pretty scenery.

"I couldn't be bothered," Jane said aloud but Rita was still going on about evening dresses and sitting at the Captain's table.

At that moment, a young waitress swooped down to take away their cups.

"I haven't finished yet and at two pounds a cup I'm going to have the last drop!" Rita protested.

"The pension doesn't go far, does it, dear?"

Rita flushed at the girl's audacity.

"My friend is not a pensioner," Jane said quietly, afraid that Rita would cause a scene.

Too late! "YOU should get your eyes tested!" she flung at the waitress as she flounced out, followed by a flustered Jane.

The day was ruined. Outside, Rita turned to her. "You're years older than me but this sort of thing never happens to you!"

Jane summoned words of sympathy. They parted at the bus-station.

Jane was glad to return to the familiar, quiet street where Ginger was still sunning himself in the front garden.

"You said he would be waiting!" A voice behind her said. It was Jim, minus his mailbag.

"You weren't out long?" It was a friendly enquiry. Jane hesitated but decided not to tell him about Rita's tantrum. Instead she asked: "Were you on the bus?"

"Been to the depot. That's my lot for the week. In

PIC: KATE DAVIES

# "Ginger goes where he's made welcome"

fact, I'll be retiring soon, just like you!"

"Women never retire," Jane answered. "There's always something to do!"

He indicated Ginger.

"Nice cat you've got. Do you know he visits me?"

Jane felt in her bag for the door key, saying: "Ginger goes where he's made welcome. He likes a cosy place and a full stomach!"

Jim agreed, saying that cats were just like people, which made them both laugh.

"If you want to come in for a coffee, you're welcome. Might even find a biscuit!" Jane offered, hoping he would accept.

"I could do with a bit of cheering up," Jim said, following the big cat into the kitchen, "I hope your friend was all right?"

Jane smiled at the kind man, sitting with Ginger on his lap.

Choosing her words carefully, she said: "Rita can be a little touchy on the subject of her age."

He nodded understandingly and dipped another biscuit into his coffee. Ginger purred and Jane couldn't help laughing.

"Is it something I've done?" Jim asked.

"Not at all. It's just that I've never known Ginger take to anyone like this before."

"I've got a confession to make," Jim looked sheepish. "He sometimes spends the night in my conservatory."

"So we actually share a cat then?"

"Well, he probably prefers to be here with you. I'm a reserve."

"Handy for me if I go on holiday," Jane said.

"You have only to ask," Jim said. "Where do you like to go on holiday?"

He seemed genuinely interested. Jane told him: "Nowhere exotic. Cornwall is my favourite place."

He raised his eyebrows in surprise. "Would you believe I've often thought of moving down there, but that's just a dream."

Jane said simply: "How amazing. It's mine, too."

# June 2010

Tuesday
## 1

Wednesday
## 2

Thursday
## 3

Friday
## 4

Saturday
## 5

Sunday
## 6

Monday
## 7

Tuesday
## 8

Wednesday
## 9

Thursday
## 10

Friday
## 11

**FIFA World Cup begins**

Saturday
## 12

Sunday
## 13

Monday
## 14

**Trooping the Colour**

Tuesday
## 15

Wednesday
## 16

Thursday
## 17

Friday
## 18

Saturday
## 19

Sunday
## 20

**Fathers' Day**

Monday
## 21

**Midsummer- the longest day**

Tuesday
## 22

| Wednesday | Sunday |
|---|---|
| 23 | 27 |
| Thursday | Monday |
| 24 | 28 |
| Friday | Tuesday |
| 25 | 29 |
| Saturday | Wednesday |
| 26 | 30 |

## Poetry corner  Heavenly hillside

The rolling hills, the swaying trees,
Flowers and grasses, dancing in the breeze.
Bees buzzing, skylarks singing, a buzzard swooping,
The wildlife around begin regrouping,
For yet another day, upon a hillside.

I lose track of life, when on top of this hill,
It's so peaceful, free and beautifully still.
No worries, no cares and the air is clean,
Upon this hill, I can just sit and dream.

Of what life could be like, if we all took the time,
To gather our thoughts and observe the sublime,
And to visit a 'hill' every once in a while.
To return to our lives – and endeavour a smile.

I sat upon this hill, looked up to the sky,
I began to think 'Why? Oh, why?'
I knew that I had to return to my home,
But all I really wanted to do was roam,
…for yet another hour upon a hillside

**Lina Rogerson, Warminster**

# My great-aunt

One of the most special relationships in my life was with my late great-aunt, Auntie Vera. Some years after her husband died in 1969, Auntie Vera moved to be nearer our family. This turned out to be a huge bonus for my sister and myself.

Not only did our great-aunt play the most exciting games, but also she owned a cat. As my sister and I were pet-less, this was luxury indeed! Tammy was an endlessly patient tabby who let us play with her for hours. I'm not so sure how much fun this was for Tammy, but my sister and I adored her. Auntie Vera also lived near an aviary, which was filled with exotic birds and she would often take us to see them. We'd never seen such a place, so we were enchanted.

Evelyn and her dear great-aunt Vera

Auntie Vera was a captivating storyteller. She would sit on the edge of my bed and the magic would begin. We'd lie spellbound while she regaled our imaginations with princes, kings, queens and princesses. Magical stories about elves, swans, dwarfs and not to mention stories based on Tammy the cat and the aviary birds. With Auntie Vera we never needed money to enjoy ourselves – just a bit of imagination. She made us crowns from cardboard and silver foil and cloaks from disused net curtains. When I grew up and began to write for children, I knew I owed a large part of my success to the inspiration of Auntie Vera.

**Evelyn Foster, Uckfield**

## Plant profile

### Convolvulus sabatius

**Height: 1.5m**
**Spread: 90cm**
**Conditions: Thrives in well-drained, light soil and full sun.**

A sensational mat-forming perennial that can climb or trail, this slightly tender species of rock bindweed is covered in purple–blue flowers during the summer months. Great in borders, baskets and containers, it has an Award of Garden Merit from the RHS. It's widely available at garden centres where it can be found in the summer bedding range.

## Health tip

### Mole check

Sun damage accumulates over the years so it's a good idea to get any moles checked by an expert. Superdrug have a team of registered nurses who can give your moles a thorough check – call 0845 678 9111 for your nearest store.

## Senior moment

Recently I was giving a workman a cup of coffee in my kitchen when he noticed a picture on my cupboard door. "That rock formation looks interesting," he said. I explained that it was the coast line where we used to live in Wales. "It's unique, gynaecologists used to come often to inspect it," I said. The man looked puzzled, then I realised what I had said! Of course, I meant geologists!

**Lorna Pope, Yorkshire**

## Fast fact

Britain's rarest flower, the Lady's Slipper Orchid, was declared extinct in 1917, but a botanist stumbled across one on a hillside in 1930. Today, this single remaining specimen is growing in a secret location somewhere in the Yorkshire Dales. Following years of research it's hoped that one day it will thrive again on our hillsides.

## Small talk

My niece had just started school and was telling us about hymn singing and prayers. When she asked, "Why do we have to say Old Men after we've finished praying?"

**Jeanne Clarke, West Midlands**

## Fashion we wore

These two photos are of me aged 20 – taken back in 1959. My future husband, Ken, made both these dresses when he was home on leave from his National Service in Germany. With no experience whatsoever and, much to my surprise, he decided just to have a go at dressmaking. He used his engineering skills to work out the pattern, cut the fabric out and made up the dresses by hand. I was delighted with the results.

**Pat Hutchinson, Leeds**

# Recipe of the week

## Ten-minute pizzas

Serves 2

- ◆ 2 thick slices wholegrain bread
- ◆ 3 tsp olive oil
- ◆ 2 tbsp sun-dried tomato paste
- ◆ 75 g (3 oz) chestnut mushrooms, sliced
- ◆ 75 g (3 oz) baby spinach
- ◆ 75 g (3 oz) ricotta or mozzarella cheese
- ◆ 1/2 tsp dried oregano
- ◆ 25 g (1 oz) Parmesan shavings
- ◆ Salt and pepper

1. Preheat the grill to a medium heat and lightly toast the bread on one side. Turn the slices over and drizzle with 1 teaspoon of the oil. Spread over the tomato paste.
2. In a frying pan, heat 1 teaspoon of the oil in a frying pan and fry the mushrooms for 5 minutes, or until softened. Scatter on the spinach, cover with a lid and turn off the heat, until the spinach starts to wilt.
3. Add the mushroom and spinach mixture to the bread.
4. Top with the cheese, season and sprinkle with oregano.
5. Grill until the cheese just starts to colour. Drizzle over the remaining oil, scatter over the Parmesan and serve immediately with a fresh green salad.

◆ **Top Tip:** Try using thinly sliced pepperoni or chorizo sausage instead of the mushrooms.

Recipe: Wholegrain Goodness, www.wholegraingoodness.com

# Life in Oz

We were one family of 2000 people on the New Australia ship bound for Australia – they called us the £10 Poms. What an adventure that six weeks on board was for myself and my two brothers. Having most of our things packed in a big crate we didn't have much to play with. Although, my Dad said he was always buying me small toy cars – a lot of them ended up overboard.

Eventually we landed in Australia to start a new beginning for us all. Mum and Dad had only £35 in their pockets and we had nowhere to live. We found a house just outside Brisbane, but life was hard. Dad worked on the bins and Mum made our clothes, as she was good at dressmaking. Our house was made of wood, not brick, with a big front and

Family fun in Australia

back yard. We had a horse, goat, cows and hens. The hens were kept for eggs and for the cooking pot. When mum said she would like a chicken for tea, dad would go just outside and get one. My little sister was born in Australia, which completed our family – two boys and two girls.

After seven happy years, we packed everything up in more big crates and came back to England. We landed home in 1962 to the worst, coldest April on record. We had no winter clothes. It was certainly a shock to the system as we were used to the hot weather in Australia.

**Laura Richards, Bristol**

## Plant profile

### Penstemon Ice Cream 'Vanilla Plum'

**Height: 50cm**
**Spread: 35cm**
**Conditions: Thrives in well-drained soil in sun or partial shade.**
Specifically bred to produce flowers that are larger than usual, this variety is compact in habit and is covered in purple, white-centred flowers all summer long. It looks great in cottage garden borders, in rustic containers, or beneath a sunny window. Try it with its colourful sisters 'Raspberry Ripple' and 'Sweet Cherry'. It's available online at www.hayloft-plants.co.uk

## Health tip

### Big-up your brain

If you think that losing your brain-power is a natural part of ageing then it's more likely to happen to you. People who think they should do badly on tests because of their age tend to, unlike people who don't buy into negative stereotypes, who do consistently better, say US researchers.

## Senior moment

During a weekend visit to relatives I went to bed a couple of hours after our hosts. Not wishing to disturb them, I crept into the bathroom in the dark. Imagine the shock when on vigorously brushing my teeth, I discovered I had mistaken Germolene for toothpaste.
**Joan Marlow, Staffordshire**

## Fast fact

Australian researchers found that the likelihood of having a body shape similar to Barbie's would be about one in 100,000. In real proportions it is thought that her waist would be somewhere around 19 inches. Not even screen goddess Brigitte Bardot could match it with her famously tiny 20-inch waist.

## Small talk

I overheard two young girls discussing holidays. One said: "Dad said, we can't have a holiday this year as the prices are too exuberant."

**Doreen Mayers, Huntingdon**

## Fashion we wore

Here's a photo of me, taken in 1945, when I was 3 years old. I think it was taken around what we used to call Whitsuntide. I remember I was bought a new outfit – something extra special for Whitsuntide and this smart little coat and hat are no exception. I know I was lucky that my parents could afford it but I did love having new clothes in fact I still do – I blame my parents and grandparents for that! I used to buy new outfits for my children at Whitsuntide too, but it's a shame, I think the tradition is no longer with us.

**Hazel V Riley, Wakefield**

## Recipe of the week

PIC: STEVE BAXTER

### Millionaires shortbread
**Makes 10-12**

Base:
◆ 200 g (8 oz) shortbread biscuits, crushed
◆ 25 g (1 oz) butter, melted

Filling:
◆ 150 g (6 oz) butter
◆ 150 g (6 oz) dark brown soft sugar
◆ 400 g (16 oz) can Carnation Condensed Milk

Topping:
◆ 200 g (8 oz) milk chocolate, melted
◆ 55 g (8 oz) white chocolate, melted

1. Line and grease a 20 cm (8 in) square baking tin. For the base, take a mixing bowl and blend the biscuits and butter. Lightly press the mixture into the tin to make an even layer and chill for 20 minutes.
2. For the filling, take a non-stick saucepan and melt the butter and sugar together. Add the condensed milk, stirring continuously, until the mixture starts to bubble. Remove from the heat immediately.
3. Spread this over the crumb base before leaving to cool. Chill for about 30 minutes.
4. Pour the melted milk chocolate over the caramel, smoothing to the edges. Place small spoonfuls of the white chocolate on top and gently swirl together to create the marbling effect. Cool and chill until the chocolate has hardened. Cut into squares.

◆ **Top Tip:** Scatter 100 g (4 oz) chopped stem ginger over the caramel layer before adding the chocolate.

Recipe: Nestlé Carnation, www.carnation.co.uk

# My domestic bliss

When I was married we had every mod-con imaginable. Most of the time I was away at sea earning my keep, but whenever I came home on leave much of my time was spent repairing those labour-saving devices. Now that I'm on my own I live a simpler life. I don't have a TV, because I'm happy listening to the radio. Or a washing machine and dryer. I do without a refrigerator and freezer and the moments of silence are bliss without that wasteful buzz. Fresh foods taste better and a few extra trips to the shops helps to keep my legs in good working order. I hate housework, so I keep it to a minimum. I'll eat almost anything and enjoy it, which is just as well since I don't have a cooker – not even a microwave. Cooking my way consists

Teeare prefers the simpler way of living

of boiling eggs or spuds and other vegetables in my electric kettle. Don't get me wrong, I'm not against cooked meals, but such a time consuming task requires a dedication that I don't have. I'm happy enough with tinned pilchards and fresh salad or cold baked beans on bread. Although full of beans, so to speak, I'm hesitant to introduce some unsuspecting lass to my domestic bliss. Cold canned beans, even with candles, are unlikely to melt her heart!

**Captain Teeare Scarrott, South Yorkshire**

## Plant profile

### Achillea millefolium 'Paprika'

**Height: 50cm**

**Spread: 35cm**

**Conditions: Thrives in most soils and a sunny position.**

A great cottage–garden plant, this variety produces masses of yellow–centred, red flowers during the summer, adding a real spicy quality to borders. It requires little attention, encourages butterflies and dries well.
Widely available from garden centres.

## Health tip
### Cherry good

Treat yourself to some fresh cherries. They contain super-powerful antioxidants, which are thought to combat ageing free radicals, say researchers from the University of Granada.

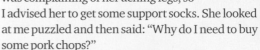

## Senior moment

My friend is getting very deaf and refuses to use her hearing aid! She was complaining of her aching legs, so I advised her to get some support socks. She looked at me puzzled and then said: "Why do I need to buy some pork chops?"

**Janine L Goddard, Gloucestershire**

## Fast fact

There are 56 different native species of butterfly living in Britain. The Brimstone, which is a yellow or pale green colour, has the longest lifespan of our native species living for up to 10 months. And, did you know that butterflies taste with their feet?

## Small talk

I was mowing the lawn in the back garden when the little daughter of my next door neighbour called over the fence: "Do you live here with your Mummy and Daddy?" "Yes," I replied. "Aren't you a big boy," she said.

**John R Stewart, London**

## Fashion we wore

I have always loved fashion and in the 1960s I was addicted to designing and making my own clothes. I made coats (complete with lining) and dresses – sometimes for the dance I was going to the next evening! I loved shopping for fabrics, especially glazed cottons – which were new – and I even had a phase of Crimplene when I was pregnant. I loved lace and fancy buttons, and often used them as inspiration for a new design. My shape has expanded a little over the years and I no longer make my own clothes. But, oh the memories that photo brings back.

**Eunice C English, by email**

## Recipe of the week

## Warm Thai chicken noodles

Serves 4

- ◆ 400 g (16 oz) chicken breast, cut into 1 cm (1/2 in) slices
- ◆ 1 tsp Thai green curry paste
- ◆ 3 tbsp cold pressed Rapeseed oil
- ◆ 200 g (8 oz) medium egg noodles
- ◆ 300 g (12 oz) beansprouts
- ◆ Zest and juice of a lime
- ◆ Salt and pepper

To serve:
- ◆ A handful of coriander, roughly chopped
- ◆ Lime wedges

1. In a mixing bowl, coat the chicken pieces with the Thai curry paste.
2. Take a large frying pan and heat one tablespoon of the oil. Fry the chicken for five minutes, or until golden and completely cooked.
3. Meanwhile, cook the egg noodles according to pack instructions. Drain and run under cold water to cool. Stir the beansprouts into the noodles.
4. In a small mixing bowl, blend the lime zest and juice with the remaining oil and season to taste. Toss into the noodles and mix well to coat evenly.
5. Divide the noodles between the serving bowls and top with the chicken. Garnish with the coriander and lime wedges and serve immediately.

Recipe: Rapeseed Oil, www.hgca.com

# Car trips to Grandma's

I was the youngest of four children and the only girl. We weren't very well off, but we did have an old car and we were also lucky enough to have a television set during the late 1950s. We lived in Nottingham but our Grandma lived in Lincoln and we made regular trips to see her. We'd all bundle into the car and wrapped in blankets in the boot was our precious cargo – the television set! Grandma had an aerial, but no television, so she was always thrilled to watch whatever offering was on the box. The Ford Popular would be put into reverse and we'd set off backwards down the drive, Dad trying to miss the brick gatepost.

In the summertime the car got very hot, but if I tried to take off my cardigan my brothers would

Janet aged nine years

grumble and moan their displeasure at me invading their space. As usual a tussle would ensue. Dad would threaten and our Mother's hand would then proceed to flap about between the front seats trying to catch whatever bare flesh it could come into contact with. One of us would accidentally nudge Dad's seat, which was an absolute no-no when he was driving. The car would be brought to a standstill and a very angry face turned on us. Threats and promises were traded and a grudging truce was agreed from the rear seat. Then we'd be back on the road to the sounds of Mrs Dale's Diary over the airwaves.

**Janet Carter, Lincoln**

## Plant profile

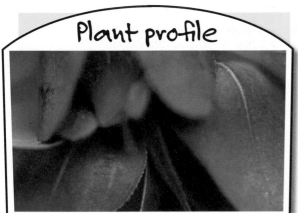

### Cerinthe major 'Purpurascens'

**Height: 60cm**
**Spread: 50cm**
**Conditions: Thrives in a sunny position on light, well-drained soils.**

A real trend-setting plant, this hardy annual produces fleshy blue-green leaves, mottled with white, and rich purple-blue flowers within sea blue bracts. Although it self-seeds freely, the seedlings are so recognisable that you can either leave them where they are, transplant them elsewhere or give them away. Seeds are widely available from garden centres and should be sown in spring.

## Health tip

### Stay cool

If the weather is hotting up avoid heat stroke, which can be fatal, by slowing down and avoiding strenuous activities, drinking plenty of water and investing in a fan to keep you cool. If you feel ill see your GP immediately.

## Senior moment

I felt quite an idiot in a shop when I asked for some chopped trousers instead of chopped tomatoes.

**Pam Musa, Essex**

## Fast fact

You may think you're being green, but using the half load programme on your washing machine still uses more than half of the water and energy than a full load. Instead save some pennies and do your bit for the environment by waiting until the laundry basket is full before doing a wash.

## Small talk

Meeting a friend in the hairdressers, she told me what her granddaughter had said to her while she was changing her trousers: "Oh Grandma, you have lovely legs. All my favourite colours – green, yellow and purple."

**Marica Rogers, Mid Glamorgan**

## Fashion we wore

**H**ere is a photo of my husband and I taken on our honeymoon in Llandudno in 1951. My suit was grey and the blouse, which I made myself, mauve. The skirt was the new length in fashion at that time, about four inches below the knee. I still make suits for myself, although the jackets are a little shorter and the skirts have been replaced with trousers. Not much difference over the past 56 years really – except for the size of course – not a 24-inch waist any more.

**Jean Lister, Halifax**

## Recipe of the week

### Broad beans and red pepper crostini
**Serves 4**

- ◆ 3 red peppers, halved and deseeded
- ◆ 250 g (10 oz) frozen broad beans
- ◆ 3 tbsp balsamic vinegar
- ◆ 3 tbsp extra virgin olive oil
- ◆ 2 cloves garlic, crushed
- ◆ Salt and pepper
- ◆ 8 slices of sourdough or ciabatta bread
- ◆ 150 g (6 oz) ricotta cheese

1. Preheat the oven to 180°C/350°F/Gas Mark 4. Dry roast the peppers for 30-40 minutes, or until they are soft and tinged with a bit of colour.
2. Meanwhile, take a medium saucepan and boil the broad beans for 4-5 minutes, or until tender. Transfer to a mixing bowl and add the vinegar, oil and garlic. Season to taste and leave to marinate.
3. Once the peppers are cooked, leave to cool slightly before peeling them and slicing thinly lengthways. Add them to the broad beans and leave to marinate for an hour, if possible.
4. Just before serving, preheat the grill to medium. Brush the bread on one side with olive oil and grill until toasted. Top each slice with a generous spoonful of the bean and pepper mixture and crumble the ricotta on top.
5. Finish with a sprinkling of pepper and serve immediately.

◆ **Top Tip:** The beans and peppers can be made up to one day in advance and chilled until ready to eat.

Recipe: British Beans and Peas, www.tastesofsummer.co.uk

# I remember Laura Ashley dresses

BY: MARION CLARKE

Floral cotton pinafore dresses, white Victorian blouses with pin tucks and ruffles, long skirts and yards of crisp broderie anglaise trim – Laura Ashley's romantic designs came as a welcome relief after years of the ultra-modern mini.

Thrilled at the opportunity to look womanly again, girls flocked to the first Laura Ashley shop when it opened in Pelham Street, South Kensington in 1968. The look was a vintage one that harked back to an earlier, more demure, era when you didn't need to be as skinny as Twiggy or have legs up to your shoulders to be in fashion. Laura Ashley clothes were unashamedly pretty and flattering to less-than-perfect figures.

## Unashamedly pretty and flattering to less-than-perfect figures

The film Butch Cassidy and the Sundance Kid was pulling in cinema audiences and girls wanted to look as gloriously frilly and feminine as Katharine Ross riding on the crossbar of Paul Newman's bike to the tune of Raindrops Keep Falling on my Head. A Laura Ashley dress was the answer to the dream.

The Laura Ashley success story began in a humble way when, inspired by a display of handicrafts at the Victoria and Albert Museum, Laura looked for suitable fabrics to make her own patchwork. Unable to find any, she designed her own flowery patterns which her husband, Bernard, printed on a silk screen printing machine in their Pimlico flat.

The couple began producing printed scarves which they sold to department stores like John Lewis, trading to begin with under the name of Ashley Mountney. After changing the name and opening their own retail outlet, the company's product range rapidly expanded from scarves, napkins and table mats to clothes and perfume and, eventually, to furnishings and wallpaper.

One American visitor to London in the early 1970s was inspired by the window of a Laura Ashley

*PIC REX FEATURES*

Unashamedly pretty with lacy petticoats.

shop that was filled with huge black and white photos of classically lovely women dressed with elegant simplicity, holding milk cans and pails in rustic settings.

Sadly, after Laura died of a brain haemorrhage following a fall downstairs in 1985, the brand was never quite the same again – but her legacy lives on in the memories of devoted customers who still write lyrically about her Emma perfume and 'wonderful white cotton blouses with ruffles around the neck' and 'a bright blue corduroy pinafore dress with tiny, dark blue flowers all over it'.

# Quiz of the month

All these events took place in the month of June over the past 60 years, but can you arrange them in the order that they happened?

PIC: REX FEATURES

**D** The body of a top Italian banker, Roberto Calvi, has been found hanging from Blackfriars Bridge in London. Known as God's banker for his links with the Vatican, Calvi was a central figure in a complex web of international fraud and intrigue.

**E** Seventy-seven people have been killed and many others injured when two cars collided on the race-track and crashed into the spectators' stand at Le Mans in north-west France.

**F** Secretary of State for War, John Profumo, has resigned from government, admitting he lied to Parliament about his relationship with a call girl.

**G** Queen Elizabeth II has been crowned at a coronation ceremony in Westminster Abbey in London.

**H** Pope John Paul II has held a private meeting with Lech Walesa, the founder and leader of Solidarity, Poland's independent trade union movement.

**I** Opposition is growing to Education Secretary Margaret Thatcher's plans to end free school milk for children over the age of seven.

**J** Nelson Mandela is jailed for life in South Africa for his part in the anti-apartheid movement.

**K** More than one million people have lined the streets of London to watch the Royal Family on their way to St Paul's at the start of the Queen's Silver Jubilee celebrations.

**L** Cricketing star Ian Botham has become the first man in the history of the game to score a century and take eight wickets in one innings of a Test match.

**M** Conservative Prime Minister, Margaret Thatcher, has been celebrating her third general election win. The victory makes her the first Prime Minister for more than 160 years to win three successive terms of office.

**N** All 118 people on board a flight from London Heathrow to Brussels have died when the airliner crashed minutes after take-off.

**O** A controversial new book by author Andrew Morton claims that Princess Diana attempted suicide on several occasions over the last decade and portrays her as a deeply depressed and unstable character.

**P** A bomb has exploded at the Houses of Parliament, causing extensive damage and injuring 11 people.

News stories taken from http://news.bbc.co.uk/onthisday/

**A** European football's governing body, UEFA, has banned English clubs from playing in Europe, following the riot at the Heysel stadium in which 39 people died.

**B** The government has announced it will introduce a blood-alcohol limit for drivers. Anyone found to be driving over the set limit will be penalised in the hope it will make roads safer.

**C** BBC Radio and commercial stations have broadcast the first live transmission from the House of Commons.

Answer: G) 1953, E) 1955, F) 1963, J) 1964, B) 1965, I) 1971, N) 1971, P) 1974, C) 1975, K) 1977, L) 1978, D) 1982, H) 1983, A) 1985, M) 1987, O) 1992.

# July 2010

Thursday

**1**

Friday

**2**

Saturday

**3**

Sunday

**4**

American Independence Day

Monday

**5**

Tuesday

**6**

Wednesday

**7**

Thursday

**8**

Friday

**9**

Saturday

**10**

Sunday

**11**

Monday

**12**

Battle of the Boyne (Bank Holiday
Northern Ireland)

Tuesday

**13**

Wednesday

**14**

Thursday

**15**

St Swithun's Day

Friday

**16**

Saturday

**17**

Sunday

**18**

Monday

**19**

Tuesday

**20**

Wednesday

**21**

Thursday

**22**

| | |
|---|---|
| **Friday**<br>23 | **Wednesday**<br>28 |
| **Saturday**<br>24 | **Thursday**<br>29 |
| **Sunday**<br>25 | **Friday**<br>30 |
| **Monday**<br>26 | **Saturday**<br>31 |
| **Tuesday**<br>27 | |

## Poetry corner

# The lemon tree of life

As the wind of change is blowing,
Through the mists of time I see,
That life is bright and bitter,
Like the fruit of the lemon tree.

Of years I am now older,
As the seasons slip away,
I think of friends and places,
That have passed along my way.

My days of early childhood,
I dwell on more and more,
But they're left forever,
Like shells upon the shore.

Those days were hard but happy,
Filled with summer sun,
Now to secret caves and woods,
My thoughts so often run.

The world is always turning,
As in life it always will,
But of those friends and places,
Are they remaining still?

Now through my children's children,
I once again return,
Though older, am I wiser,
Or am I still to learn?

Life becomes a circle,
Filled with thoughts and memory,
But my past becomes the future,
For the seeds of the lemon tree.

**Terry White, Cadiz, Spain**

# A famous gnome

**M**y gnome family love sitting by my beautiful busy lizzies, which bloomed all last summer next to my yellow lilies. They really are a wonderful sight to see and the seeds were all bought from Woolworths – how I will miss that shop!

I only have a small garden, but I spend many happy hours pottering in it. I have a varied gnome collection and my Scottish gnome was even chosen to appear in a Cornish calendar in 2008. Named Jock, he is quite famous now. I like to think of him adorning the walls of houses across the country!

**Barbara Girling, Suffolk**

Barbara's pretty blooms from Woolworths

Spot the gnome family enjoying Barbara's garden

## Plant profile

### Zantedeschia aethiopica

**Height: 90cm**
**Spread: 90cm**
**Conditions: Thrives in moist soil in sun or partial shade. It's only half-hardy so requires frost protection during winter.**

An exquisite South African perennial, this is 'must' if you have a pond, and even if you don't – try growing it in a water–filled barrel instead. Plant it in an aquatic basket and lower it into water about 15cm deep. It produces large, heart–shaped leaves followed by showy, pure white flowers during the summer. Widely available in garden centres.

## Health tip

### Holiday Romance

If you're single and feel like indulging in a summer fling do remember to practise safe sex. Sexually transmitted infections are on the rise in the over 45s – so protect yourself by always using a condom.

## Senior moment

Our daughter came over for lunch and noticed a vegetable peeler in the cutlery drawer and said: "Oh, that's new." "Yes," I replied. "Dad and I have both tried it but it doesn't work." She inspected it and removed the plastic cover protecting the blade. It works perfectly now!

**Doreen P Cross, Warwickshire**

## Fast fact

The phrase 'green-eyed monster' is said to have been coined by William Shakespeare in his work Othello in the line 'O, beware, my lord, of jealousy; It is the green-eyed monster'. In the same play he also coined the phrase 'foregone conclusion'.

## Small talk

I asked my four-year-old grandson if he would like to brush the cats. But before I could tell him I had bought special new cat brushes, he had picked up the rather large yard brush! Poor cats, they soon disappeared.

**L Turton, Nottingham**

## Fashion we wore

I thought readers might like to see these photos from 1953. The first, my wedding outfit, was photographed after we returned from our honeymoon. It was bought at Marshall & Snellgrove in London for £50. My mother and I took the whole day off to choose a dress but this was the first one I tried on. The dress under the jacket had a halter-neck for eveningwear and the pearl earrings were homemade. The second picture is my 'going away outfit' – a blue seersucker dress costing £10 from C&A, where I also bought the inexpensive 'lampshade' hat.

**Mary Forbat, Weybridge, Surrey**

# Recipe of the week

## Chantenay dippers and dip

Serves 4

- 1 x 400 g (16 oz) can of butterbeans, drained and rinsed
- 50 g (2 oz) watercress
- 2 tbsp cold pressed Rapeseed oil, plus extra for drizzling
- Juice and zest of 1 lemon
- 1 clove garlic
- 2 tbsp chives, chopped
- Salt and pepper

To serve:
- 400 g (16 oz) Chantenay carrots, washed and scrubbed

1. In a food processor or blender, place the beans, watercress, oil, lemon juice and zest, garlic and chives and blend to a smooth puree. Season to taste.
2. Spoon into a serving bowl and drizzle over a little more oil and some black pepper. Serve with the Chantenay carrots.

◆ **Top Tip:** This dip can be made in advance and stored for up to 3 days and makes a tasty addition to any picnic hamper.

Recipe: Chantenay Carrots, www.chantenay.co.uk/

# A friendly neighbourhood

I was the eldest of two brothers born in the small village of Cowling, West Yorkshire. We lived in a terraced house with no bath or hot water, but we did have an old cast-iron gas oven. The back yard had a stone ashpit and coalplace, and an old Tippler-style toilet.

The street was very busy in those days. Milk and coal were delivered by horse and cart and the backyard ashpits were emptied weekly in this fashion also. Householders took their jugs to the milk cart and queued up waiting for them to be filled. Besides storing coal and wood in our coal place we would dig peat on Ickornshaw Moor and when it had dried out it would be stored until it was needed to burn on our fires. This summer my

Geoffrey batting with his brother Owen

granddaughter's husband, a farmer, is going to be one of the first to start peating again. As the prices of gas and electricity are now soaring and quite a few people have wood-burning stoves, history is now repeating itself.

I remember two old-time buskers sometimes used to come round in the evening and play the concertina and give us a few songs. Everyone would come out of their houses to listen to the entertainment. In the very good weather and long daylight hours people would sit on their doorsteps and chat with friends and neighbours until bedtime.

**Geoffrey Binns, West Yorkshire**

## Plant profile

### Helenium 'Indian Summer'

**Height: 90cm**
**Spread: 35cm**
**Conditions: Plant in moist, well-drained soil and a sunny position.**

No summer garden would be complete without heleniums. With vibrant daisy–like flowers in red, orange and copper, they create a fiery blaze of colour from June onwards. This variety is great at the back of a border where it will complement ornamental grasses and chrysanthemums. Widely available from garden centres.

## Health tip
### Move it

One of the biggest risk factors for osteoporosis is being lazy. The more active you are the stronger and denser your bones will be. Aim to walk, jog or dance every single day to beef-up your bones.

## Senior moment

On the way to return some DVDs, I stopped to stroke a little dog. Distracted, I dropped the DVDs through the slot. It wasn't until I got home that I realised I'd posted them in the Royal Mail post box instead of the shop's letterbox!

**Mrs R Clayton, Berkshire**

## Fast fact

The SOS Morse code signal was globally adopted on July 1, 1908. When Titanic sent out distress signals in 1912 it sent both SOS and the old CQD signals. The phrase 'Mayday', the internationally recognised code word for vessels in distress, is derived from the French 'venez m'aider' – meaning 'come help me'.

## Small talk

I went to the local community centre to play bingo, along with my sister and her seven-year-old grandson, Jack. One local lady is a regular, and I explained to Jack that she will be 100 years old this year. He looked and said: "100, she should be dead shouldn't she? Or has she come back?" Everyone around had a good laugh!

**Lyn Cuthbert, Cleveland**

## Fashion we wore

How about these two fashionable photos? The first is me as a baby, with my mum in 1937. Her coat was a fitted, double-breasted 'donkey brown' colour. The second is of me twenty years later on the catwalk. My dress was pale blue organza with white, flocked flowers, white elbow gloves, and white feathery stranded hat. The shoes were my own, black suede. What a trendy pair Mum and me were!

**Wendy Walcott, Bristol**

## Recipe of the week

### Tex–Mex nachos
**Serves 4–6**

◆ 200 g (8 oz) lightly salted tortilla chips
◆ 1 x multipack readymade chilled Mexican dips (salsa, guacamole and soured cream)
◆ 50 g (2 oz) cheddar cheese, grated

1. Preheat the grill to a high heat. Take a large shallow ovenproof dish, or plate, and empty the chips out. Gently shake dish to get an even layer.
2. Using a teaspoon, spoon the salsa sauce all over the chips, repeat with the guacamole, then the soured cream and chives dip.
3. Scatter the cheese over the top and pop under the hot grill. Cook for 2 minutes, or until the cheese has melted and the chips start browning. Serve immediately to accompany a sandwich or as a snack on its own.

◆ **Top Tip:** This snack proves popular with the grandchildren

Recipe: Bakkavor, leading producer of supermarket fresh dips

# A lasting friendship

Imagine, if you can, two four-year-old little girls pushing their tiny kittens dressed in doll's clothes along the street in their dolls' prams. Perhaps, you remember seeing these two little girls, but then it was nearly a hundred years ago that my mother Nora Jones and her best friend Hilda pushed those kittens along the streets of Edgbaston.

Sadly Hilda died in 2009, aged 98, bringing to an end a friendship that lasted 93 years. My mother celebrated her 98th birthday in April the same year. She still lives in her own house – the only help she has is with some of her

Proud Viv with her mother Nora.

housework, shopping and gardening.

She regularly attends her local Methodist Church and thoroughly enjoys outings with friends to the local golf club for lunch. Can anyone beat that – a friendship of 93 years?

**Mrs Viv Jones, Evesham**

## Plant profile

### Coreopsis 'Limerock Dream'

**Height: 50cm**
**Spread: 50cm**
**Conditions: Loves a sunny position and well-drained soil.**

A new introduction, this hardy perennial has beautiful thread–like foliage and burnt orange flowers between June and October. Extremely drought tolerant, it attracts wildlife including bees and butterflies. Great in a cottage–garden style planting scheme. Available online at www.hayloft-plants.co.uk

## Health tip
### Daydream believer

If you've got a problem to solve then indulge in a bit of daydreaming. A study from the University of British Columbia found that letting your mind wander kick-starts its solution finding areas and helps you to deal with those troubling issues.

## Senior moment

Halfway through the morning I realised I was very tired but I couldn't think why. I found out that evening when I went to take my usual tablet to help me sleep. It was missing – but my morning tablet was still there. I had taken my night time tablet in the morning by mistake!

**Mrs L Evans, Staffs**

## Fast fact

We spend around £2.4 billion on electricity to power lighting in our homes each year. Just by switching to energy-saving light bulbs you could save yourself up to £50 a year. If every UK household installed just three compact fluorescent light bulbs in place of traditional bulbs, enough energy would be saved in a year to supply street lighting across the UK.

## Small talk

My grandson Christopher, aged three, was staying with me for the weekend when he whispered to me: "Nana, give me your teeth from your cabinet because the tooth fairy hasn't been to you. Don't worry, I'll put them under my pillow and I'll give you the money she leaves me."

**Pam Gittins, Wirral**

## Fashion we wore

Here are a couple of pictures of my parents. The first is of my mum, Josephine (on the right) and her best friend Pat Baker, in Trafalgar Square, London on VE night 1945. They were very excited, and Mum had borrowed her mother's best 'fun' fur coat to wear (I don't think Nan knew). They were both under 16, but I think the clothes make them seem much older. The second is a photo of my dad, Colin, in his best suit and favourite pair of shoes. It was taken in 1945 and I'm not sure where he was going – maybe to paint the town red! I just love his wide tie and two-tone shoes. Dad still lives in the same house, but the garden looks rather different.

**Julia Lovell, by email**

## Recipe of the week

PIC: STEVE BAXTER

### Coffee crème bûlées
**Makes 6**

- ◆ 568 ml (1 pint) carton whipping cream
- ◆ 2 tsp Nescafé Espresso coffee powder
- ◆ 4 large egg yolks
- ◆ 170 g (7 oz) tube Carnation Condensed Milk
- ◆ Caster sugar, to glaze

1. Preheat the oven to 150°C/300°F/Gas Mark 2.
2. In a small saucepan, gently bring the cream and coffee powder up to the boil. Meanwhile, in a large bowl, mix the egg yolks and condensed milk.
3. Remove the coffee cream from the heat and gradually whisk into the egg yolk mixture. Pour into six ramekins or oven-proof coffee cups.
4. Carefully place the ramekins in a deep roasting tin and fill the tin with enough boiling water to come two thirds up the sides of the dishes. Cover with foil and bake for 40 minutes, or until just set. Remove from the oven and place the ramekins on a rack to cool to room temperature. Chill before serving.
5. To glaze the brûlées, preheat the grill to high. Sprinkle a thin layer of caster sugar over each dish, ensuring they are completely covered. Place under the grill for 5–6 minutes, or until the sugar has melted to a golden brown – this stage needs constant observation. Cool slightly before serving.

◆ **Top Tip:** This recipe can be made up to 2 days in advance and glazed at the last minute.

Recipe: Nestlé Carnation, www.carnation.co.uk

# It's all about age

**M**y first entanglement with the unfathomable sex came after I had just turned 11 years old. My best friend Keith, who was 14, lived next door. He was of the age where his hormones were rampant, but I was more interested in watching cartoons.

We were in town one day and Keith suddenly stopped and whispered in a conspiratorial voice: "Don't look over there." "Where," I replied as he gestured with his eyebrows towards the chip shop. Sitting outside on the wall were two girls from our school and Keith informed me he fancied the brunette. He came up with the plan that he would

Paul with the ladies in his life.

go over and say I fancied her friend and then we could all go out together. It sounded simple.

As I slowly approached I could hear Keith finishing off the chat up line: "So if you fancy him we can all go out as a foursome." The other girl took one look at me and asked how old I was. I was so stunned that a girl had actually spoken directly at me I told her my real age. She was 14, so obviously her answer was no. As Keith and I walked sheepishly away I heard him swear under his breath. Fearing I'd let him down I offered: "Do you think it would have been better if I'd have said twelve?" I didn't see much of Keith from that day.

**Paul Simpson, Morecambe**

## Plant profile

### Cosmidium 'Brunette'

**Height: 55cm**
**Spread: 10cm**
**Conditions: Thrives in well-drained soil and a sunny position.**
A hardy annual, this heirloom variety has been cultivated since the 19th century. It produces yellow-edged, mahogany flowers and finely-divided leaves on slender stems all summer. Simply prepare the ground well and, once you've created a fine tilth, sow it where you want it to flower. Thin the seedlings if necessary.

## Health tip
### See the funny side

A sense of humour could increase your chances of pulling through a health dip. Norwegian doctors found that patients who could laugh at their troubles were more likely to see their health improve.

## Senior moment

I was standing behind a lady in a café queue waiting to be served. She said to the assistant: "I'm sorry, I forgot to pick up a tray." The assistant replied: "You're holding it under your arm madam."

**Mrs Cook, Stafford**

## Fast fact

Pablo Picasso's birth name was Pablo Diego José Francisco de Paula Juan Nepomuceno María de los Remedios Cipriano de la Santísima Trinidad Ruiz y Picasso. Phew, now that's a mouthful!

## Small talk

I asked our grandson, Cade, who is two years old, if he'd like a plum from the fruit bowl. "No thank you," he replied, "they're dirty." Then we realised he was used to golden plums and the ones in the basket were purple.

**Mrs V A Marshall, Scunthorpe, North Lincs**

## Fashion we wore

I thought readers might like to see some photos of my favourite outfits over the years. The first, taken in 1962 in Holland I'm wearing a white dress, which was made for my confirmation. It was a cotton seersucker material and didn't need ironing. The second, taken in 1985, I'm wearing the same dress with the addition of a trendy shawl and hat. I still have the dress, in fact, but I'm not sure if I could get in it now though! The third picture was taken in Portsmouth in 1959. I'm wearing a dress that I made myself – white cotton with blue polka dots. I loved this dress and always felt really pretty when I wore it.

**Pamela Patten, Portugal**

# Recipe of the week

## Monster mushroom burgers

Serves 4

- ◆ 4 large Portobello or large field mushrooms
- ◆ 2 tbsp olive oil
- ◆ 1 clove garlic, crushed
- ◆ Salt and pepper
- ◆ 4 crusty ciabatta rolls

To serve:
- ◆ 100 g (4 oz) lettuce
- ◆ 2 tomatoes, sliced
- ◆ 200 g (8 oz) homus

1. Preheat the grill to high (or light the barbeque).
2. In a large mixing bowl, place the mushrooms and add the oil, garlic and seasoning. Toss gently until the mushrooms are evenly coated. Leave to marinate for at least 10 minutes.
3. Cook the mushrooms for 8-10 minutes, or until browned on both sides and tender when tested with a fork. Transfer to a plate, topside down and keep warm. Meanwhile, slice the roll in half and toast under the grill or on the barbecue.
4. Spread a generous dollop of homus on each cut side and place a mushroom in each bap. Fill with the lettuce and tomato slices and serve immediately.

Recipe: Mushroom Bureau, www.mushroom–uk.com

# Step back in time

I recall a past sermon by the vicar about looking forward and not backwards. He referred to forty and fifty year olds, both men and women, trying to recapture their lost youth by visiting nightclubs and jigging about with the youngsters. I understand the point of the sermon, but I look back with joy. I'm intrigued by the past – not just my youth, but also the lives of my ancestors.

Last February my old school celebrated its centenary year and I was reunited with old school friends from more than 50 years ago. We shared an immediate affinity that blossomed and there were no inhibitions or pretences. Chatting about the old times is better for you than any medicine. Even health talk of new hips and

Mary with her mother and father – looking back is a joy.

knees couldn't stop the fun!

We danced the quickstep and foxtrot around the sprung floor at Spennymoor Rink to Glen Miller. We straightened our black seamed stockings. Our circular skirts were stiff and scratchy with yards of net and our winkle picker shoes crammed our toes together. We reminisced about the excitement of youth, the freedom and the possibilities.

Surely nostalgia is good for the soul. It's a feeling and a connection. I embrace my past and will pass my memories on to my children and grandchildren. Looking back is so therapeutic – I love it!

**Mary Grant, Saltburn**

## Plant profile

### Verbena 'Sissinghurst'

**Height: 15cm**
**Spread: 70cm**
**Conditions: Thrives in well-drained compost and sun or partial shade.**

Producing clusters of salmon–pink flowers on trailing stems, this is a great container plant. Mix it with Argyranthemum 'Pompanet Pink' and Nemesia 'Karoo Soft Blue' and you'll enjoy colour all summer.

All three plants are available as the Creative Images Collection at www.hayloft-plants.co.uk

## Health tip
### Book a check up

See your local pharmacist for a medication review. Boots, Lloyds Pharmacies and many independent chemists offer free medicine checks. Your pharmacist will make sure you understand your medication and how to take it and check your doses for you.

## Senior moment

My husband and I were shopping in a department store. As we passed a mirror he commented that he'd just seen a man wearing the same cap as him. He was looking at his own reflection!

**Mrs Quinnell, North Herts**

## Fast fact

On July 22, 1933 the first recorded sighting of the Loch Ness monster was made by Mr Spicer and his wife who claimed they saw a large lumbering body crossing the road yards from the water.

## Small talk

When my daughter's dog, Tess, died her ashes were buried in the garden. When I was visiting I said to my grandson: "What lovely daffodils are under the tree." "Yes Nan," he replied, "That's where they burnt Tessie's eyelashes."

**Maureen Coates, Cardiff**

## Fashion we wore

This is a photograph of me and my friend Eileen Billing, taken in 1944 when we were both 14. We lived in London and had gone to Margate for the day to cheer ourselves up as she had just lost her brother in the RAF, and I had just lost my father at the battle of Monte Cassino in Italy. I'm on the right – wearing the only dress I owned at the time – blue with frilly shoulders. We're standing beside one of the novelty 'head-through-hole' backdrops that photographers used on the seafront, but we couldn't afford to have our photos taken in the holes provided!

**Kitty Baxter, by email**

# Recipe of the week

## Pear and berry cobbler
### Serves 6

- 6 ripe pears, peeled, cored and diced
- 250 g (10 oz) frozen berries
- 75 g (3 oz) golden caster sugar
- 100 g (4 oz) plain flour
- 125 g (5 oz) wholemeal flour
- 50 g (2 oz) rolled porridge oats, plus 1 tbsp for sprinkling
- 25 g (1 oz) golden caster sugar
- 1 tsp bicarbonate of soda
- 1 tsp baking powder
- ½ tsp salt
- 50 g (2 oz) butter, melted
- 240 ml (10 oz) buttermilk

1. Preheat the oven to 180°C/350°F/Gas Mark 4. In a large saucepan, mix the pears and berries with the sugar, until evenly coated. Bring to the boil and simmer uncovered for 15 minutes. Spoon into an ovenproof dish.
2. In a large mixing bowl, stir together the dry ingredients. Make a well in the centre and add the butter and buttermilk then mix together to form a sticky dough.
3. Drop large spoonfuls of the dough onto the fruit, scatter over the reserved oats then bake for 30–35 minutes, or until the crust is golden brown and the fruit is tender. Serve immediately with a scoopful of vanilla ice cream, or clotted cream.

◆ **Top tip:** If you have difficulty sourcing buttermilk mix together a 150 g (6 oz) carton of low fat yoghurt and 100 ml (4 fl oz) milk for a good substitute.

Recipe: Wholegrain Goodness, www.wholegraingoodness.com

# I remember nylon stockings

## BY: MARION CLARKE

**B**efore the arrival of the mini skirt in the 1960s made the invention of tights absolutely essential (thank you, inventor Allen Gant Senior), all women over the age of 12 wore stockings. Being given your first pair of nylons and suspender belt was a rite of passage that marked the end of childhood and those carefree days when you just tugged on a comfy pair of socks in the morning.

Nylons were delicate items, all too easily snagged even as you carefully extracted them from their crackly cellophane package. 'One simple but excellent form of stocking insurance is well-manicured nails' advised Good Housekeeping magazine, smugly. But however carefully you handled your precious hosiery, unsightly ladders were inevitable. A bad ladder was almost impossible to mend so we tried to limit the damage by applying clear nail polish to prevent its speedy upward progress.

Another challenge presented by nylon stockings

## Another challenge was keeping seams straight

was trying to keep those seams straight. This involved a lot of twisting round, trying to check the backs of your legs every time you passed a mirror. And before the invention of Lycra© in the 1960s, fully-fashioned stockings (as they were called) had no stretch in them so they tended to get baggy and wrinkly, especially if your legs were on the skinny side.

While we all dreamed of looking like Jane, the glamour girl in the Daily Mirror who put the 'strip' into strip cartoons, and usually wore little more than cami-knickers and hose, in reality we were more like Andy Capp's wife Flo, a fore-runner of Nora Batty, famous for her baggy stockings. (Although Flo and Nora probably wore sensible lisle stockings which were made of cotton and almost guaranteed to sag around the ankles.)

Last but not least was the problem of keeping your stockings up. You could choose between a suspender

If only we could all have worn stockings like Sophia Loren!

PIC: REX FEATURES

belt (made of cotton which, again, wasn't stretchy so it cut uncomfortably into your middle) or an elastic roll-on which held you in a vice-like grip from the waist down. All too often, suspenders snapped under the strain of being tugged in opposite directions and had to be replaced with a safety pin, halfway through the day.

When tights came into the shops, men dismissed them as 'passion killers' but we girls were only too glad to say goodbye to suspender belts and stockings – and that thigh-chilling gap in between!

# Quiz of the month

All these events took place in the month of July over the past 60 years, but can you arrange them in the order that they happened?

PIC: REX FEATURES

**F** Jim Morrison, the lead singer of American rock group The Doors, has died in Paris aged 27.

**G** Michael Fagan, 31, scaled the walls around Buckingham Palace and shinned up the drainpipe to the private apartments. He spent ten minutes talking to the Queen in her bedroom before being arrested.

**H** Ronald Biggs – a member of the gang who carried out the Great Train Robbery – has escaped from Wandsworth Prison.

**I** Ruth Ellis has been hanged having been found guilty of shooting her lover, 25-year-old racing driver David Blakely.

**J** The birth of the world's first 'test tube baby', Louise Brown, has been announced in Manchester.

**K** The British Prime Minister, Harold Macmillan, has made an optimistic speech telling the people of Britain that they, 'have never had it so good'.

**L** The chairman of the Palestinian Liberation Organisation, Yasser Arafat, has returned to the Gaza Strip after 27 years in exile.

**M** The former Gestapo chief in Lyon, Klaus Barbie, has been sentenced to life in prison for crimes against humanity.

**N** The Live Aid concert, for the starving in Africa, has raised a global total of £30m.

**O** The Olympic Games has opened in the Spanish city of Barcelona with all countries present for the first time in modern history.

**P** Thousands of Turkish troops have invaded northern Cyprus after last-minute talks in the Greek capital, Athens, failed to reach a solution.

News stories taken from http://news.bbc.co.uk/onthisday/

**A** A massive fire has devastated large parts of York Minster causing an estimated £1m damage.

**B** American Neil Armstrong becomes the first man to walk on the Moon.

**C** American tennis player Arthur Ashe has become the first black man to win the Wimbledon men's singles' championship.

**D** Crowds of 600,000 people filled the streets of London to catch a glimpse of Prince Charles and Lady Diana Spencer on their wedding day.

**E** England have won the football World Cup for the first time since the tournament began.

ANSWER: I) 1955, K) 1957, H) 1965, E) 1966, B) 1969, F) 1971, P) 1974, C) 1975, J) 1978, D) 1981, G) 1982, A) 1984, N) 1985, M) 1987, O) 1992, L) 1994

# The future's bright

BY: JOANNA BARNDEN

## Nancy's stint as a fortune-teller has an unforeseen outcome!

"Ta Dah!" I cried, stumbling out of the bathroom in a swirl of Oxfam-bought frills and flounces. "Gypsy Daffodil Lee!"

I looked in my full-length mirror and barely recognised myself. With my ash-blonde curls hidden beneath a purple silk scarf, gold hoops in my ears and mascara caking my eyelashes, I looked exotic and unfamiliar.

When my daughter Lucy had talked me into using my grandmother's old tarot cards to tell fortunes at the school's summer fête I'd agreed reluctantly, but now I was beginning to see the possibilities.

I thought, 'Oh, Phillip, if you could see me now!' and glanced out of the window to our small orchard where I'd buried my husband's ashes over a year ago.

## I was a dad hand with the tarot cards and reading palms

I'd stood there, day after long winter day, wrapped in a fog of memories. And it was there that, last spring, I'd seen the first daffodil unfold and realised it was possible to push your head up out of the dark, hard soil of grief. I felt a fondness for the tough, determined little flower.

The daffodil had inspired me to live again. With one last glance at the orchard, I set off for my grandchildren's school where the good ladies of the PTA greeted me with delight. They showed me to my tent, which had been decked out with brilliant silks and satins to match my new persona.

By the time I sat down behind my little table I felt very much in character. I laid out my cards and my crystal 'ball' (a round glass vase which looked very effective upside-down with a tea-light flickering inside), hid the palmistry crib sheet I'd got off the internet and was ready for business.

Gypsy Daffodil Lee proved instantly popular.

I was a bit nervous that my 'clients' would expect too much of my dubious skills but I was advertised as a 'bit of fun with the future' and I soon got into the swing of it. After years of doing my party piece at family gatherings, I was a dab hand with the tarot cards and reading palms was simple. The crystal ball was harder but I soon found that a brief chat with the person perched on the stool opposite made it pretty clear what they wanted from life.

It gave me quite a thrill to see their faces light up when I plucked their dreams out of thin air.

The sun was beating down, making me hot and sticky. Outside, I could hear children laughing, adults chattering happily and snatches of a crackly voice announcing the hay-tossing competition and the results of 'guess the name of the teddy'.

I began to long for a break but people were still queuing up. I sent a lad out grinning at the promise of true love in the offing and a tired-looking young mum went away looking hopeful at the idea of an 'unexpected break'.

I was looking forward to going home and putting my feet up when a voice said: "Hello?"

I knew who it was the moment he stepped into the tent. He was older than when I'd last seen him but he was still unmistakably Bill Tompkins. I'd heard he was moving back to the area after losing his wife, so it was no great surprise – but it did offer me a perfect opportunity to impress.

"I see a recent move," I told him solemnly as we placed our hands on the glowing crystal ball. Hamming it up a little, and enjoying myself again now, I added: " And I see a return."

He nodded, looking faintly surprised.

"You've known loss." He cast his eyes down and I hurried on. "But now it's time for renewal, for reaffirmation of the good things in life."

His eyes met mine, shiny with pain.

"How do you know?" he asked.

"I've been there," I admitted, before quickly snatching my Gypsy Daffodil Lee persona back into place.

I went on: "I see family. Love. And maybe remorse."

He was staring intently at me now. "Remorse?"

"Yes, a deep-seated remorse…" He looked alarmed… "For pulling a little girl's pigtails – which she hated, anyway."

PIC KATE DAVIES

# I met his eyes and something unexpected happened

"Nancy Simpson!"

I blinked at hearing my maiden name.

"Nancy Shaw now," I told him. "I'm a widow."

"That's how you knew about…"

"About loss, yes – and about renewal, too."

I met his eyes and something unexpected happened: a tantalising moment of hopes and dreams. Or was that just an illusion left over from my other visitors? Beyond the tent, I could hear the clatter of stalls being taken down and the wails of children being rounded up to go home.

"I'm about done here," I said to Bill. "Do you think the WI is still serving tea?"

"I'm sure of it. My daughter's in charge and she's a bossy lass. She'll have them there to the bitter end!"

"Mine's the same," I laughed. "That's how I ended up doing this!"

But I had to admit to myself that I'd had a good time and the day was ending on an unexpected high.

"Let me buy you a cup of tea and cake," Bill smiled. "You've earned it."

Packing away my tarot cards and crystal ball, I shook my hair loose and stepped out into the sunshine with Bill.

Gypsy Daffodil Lee had, it seemed, brought me a new friend – and who knew what the future might hold?

# August 2010

Sunday
**1**

Monday
**2**

Tuesday
**3**

Wednesday
**4**

Thursday
**5**

Friday
**6**

Saturday
**7**

Sunday
**8**

Monday
**9**

Tuesday
**10**

Wednesday
**11**

Thursday
**12**

Friday
**13**

Saturday
**14**

Sunday
**15**

Monday
**16**

Tuesday
**17**

Wednesday
**18**

Thursday
**19**

Friday
**20**

Saturday
**21**

Sunday
**22**

| Monday 23 | Saturday 28 |
| --- | --- |
| Tuesday 24 | Sunday 29 |
| Wednesday 25 | Monday 30 — Summer Bank Holiday |
| Thursday 26 | Tuesday 31 |
| Friday 27 | |

## Poetry corner

Hands that are tiny,
Very small and sweet,
Hands that can quicken
Your very heartbeat.
Hands that can make you
A wobbly school 'pot',
Treasured forever,
It means such a lot.
Hands that can comfort
With power to heal,
Hands that can cook well
And bring you a meal.
Hands that are wrinkled
And crippled with pain,
A lifetime of caring,
And now on the wane.
Hands that have worked hard,
All along life's way,
Are raised in a blessing,
At each end of a day.

**Sheila Sidebottom, Middlesex**

# Helping hands

PIC: REX FEATURES

# A haven to relax in

**D**uring the Seventies our garden was rather neglected, but it proved to be a haven for our young daughter who would play with her friends on the swing and slide and splash about in her paddling pool. By the middle of the Eighties we'd moved out all the playthings, but this left us with an empty unattractive and somewhat open garden. I was determined to give it a face-lift and make a colourful and private garden that would be a haven for us to relax in. Over the years, with the help of our friends and relatives, who gave me cuttings and plants for birthday presents, I persevered to make it as it is today – a beautiful colourful cottage garden.

**Irene Purslow, Birmingham**

Irene's garden over the decades... 1970, 1980, 1990 and as it is today.

## Plant profile

### Phlomis fruticosa

**Height: 1m**
**Spread: 1.5m**
**Conditions: Thrives in well-drained or sandy soils and enjoys a sunny position.**

A really handsome Mediterranean species, this robust silver shrub is great in dry, south–facing borders and copes well with exposed coastal gardens. Evergreen – it produces yellow flowers during the summer. Prune it after flowering to prevent it becoming leggy at the base, and take cuttings so you can replace old plants every few years. Available from garden centres, it has an Award of Garden Merit from the RHS.

## Health tip

### You shall have a fishy

Add salmon and other oily fish to your weekly shopping list and you could reduce your risk of heart failure say European scientists. The omega-3 fatty acids in the fish help to lower levels of fat in your blood and reduce blood pressure.

## Senior moment

I found a black mark behind the sink in the bathroom. I spent quite a while trying to remove it with all sorts of cleaners and bleach but nothing worked. I went into the bathroom later without the light on and realised I had spent some time tying to clean off a shadow!

**Mary Hargreaves, North Yorkshire**

## Fast fact

The next Olympic Games will take place from July 27 to August 12, 2012, when London will officially become the first city to host the games three times. The programme will now feature 26 sports in 34 different venues, following the committee's decision to drop baseball and softball.

## Small talk

Our grandson James was looking forward to his first school trip. He was trying to decide which game to take for the journey. He couldn't make his mind up: "Oh, I know," he said, "I'll just take a nap." He's just like his granddad!

**Mrs L M Hanson, Lancs**

## Fashion we wore

Here are two photos of my Mum, Joan. The first was taken when she was all ready for her first dance at the village hall near to her place of work in Sussex. Her dress was made of satin in pale lavender with a darker trim. She was then a teenager, aged about 14 or 15. The second was taken a few years ago, on her way to her grandson's wedding. I think she looks great for her age.

**S Glue, West Sussex**

# Recipe of the week

## Chickpea, shallot and feta salad
Serves 4

- ◆ 12 shallots, peeled and cut in half
- ◆ 2 cloves garlic, whole and unpeeled
- ◆ 25vg (1 oz) butter, diced
- ◆ Salt and pepper
- ◆ 400 g (16 oz) can of chickpeas, drained and rinsed
- ◆ 200 g (8 oz) feta cheese, crumbled
- ◆ 100 g (4 oz) lettuce leaves
- ◆ 3 tbsp extra virgin olive oil
- ◆ 2 tbsp sherry vinegar
- ◆ 1 tsp honey
- ◆ I small bunch flat leaf parsley, roughly chopped

1. Preheat the oven to 200°C/400°F/Gas Mark 6. Place the shallots in a roasting tin, cut side up, dot with the butter and season well. Add the unpeeled whole garlic cloves and roast for 15 minutes, or until the onions are soft and golden.
2. Remove from the tin and keep to one side while you make the dressing in the roasting tin. Squeeze the garlic out of its skin and mash with a fork. Add the oil, vinegar and honey and using a small whisk combine with the mashed roast garlic, scraping the bottom of the tin to get off all the caramelized shallot juices. Add the chopped parsley and season to taste.
3. Add the chickpeas to the roasting tin and toss to evenly coat in the dressing.
4. In a serving dish arrange the lettuce with the roast shallots and pour over the chickpeas and dressing. Top with the crumbled feta and serve immediately.

Recipe: UK Shallots, www.ukshallot.com

# Our Morris

I was four years old when the war came to an end. Throughout those confined years my father's Morris 12 hadn't moved from the wooden garage at the side of our house in West Heath. The engine rotor-arm was locked away at King's Norton Police Station for the duration of the war to foil any invading German soldiers should they have attempted to make off with our motor.

My parents promised that after the war we'd ride to Aunty's house on the other side of Birmingham. Day after day I'd ask: "Is the war over yet?" My mother never tired of explaining it would soon be over. Too excited to wait I used to play in the stationary car, clambering in with my dolls and

Gail and her father with their beloved Morris 12

sitting on the smooth, green leather seats. I'd place my dolls on the back and I'd sit in the driver's bucket-seat, bolstered by three cushions so I could see out.

Then one day father announced that the rotor-arm had been retrieved from the police station and we could all climb aboard for the long promised ride. Our first outing was to go see the shops all lit up in Birmingham at night. Due to the blackout shop owners hadn't been allowed to light up their shops. Stuffed in like sardines we set off for the big city. I'd never experienced such excitement, in my eyes 'Town' was like a Fairy Land. As the wartime restrictions eased we had many more journeys in our lovely Morris 12.

**Gail Hare, Solihull**

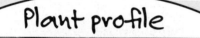
## Health tip
### Throw a party

Gather all your friends and family together for a party and you could boost your wellbeing. Australian researchers found that people with a good social network live longer and are healthier.

## Senior moment

Making a Dundee cake I mixed the ingredients together then added the fruits. Not taking much notice that the mixing was somewhat easy, I poured the mixture into a baking tin just as my eyes caught sight of an unopened packed of flour!

**Bill Addison, Stockport**

## Fast fact

The origin of the superstition surrounding Friday the 13th can be traced to Norse mythology. Friday is named after Frigga, the free-spirited goddess of love and fertility who was later banished and labelled a witch. It was believed that every Friday, she and eleven other witches, plus the devil – a gathering of thirteen – got together and plotted ill turns of fate for the coming week.

## Small talk

When I went to see my grandson in his school play, I was disappointed that there was no sign of him. Later, I asked him what part he had played. He said happily, "Didn't you see me? It was my hand that drew the curtain."

**Mary King, Cleveland**

## Fashion we wore

**H**ere are a few snaps of me aged 17 in 1959. I was a bit of a poser and the boyfriend I had at the time loved taking photos. The first was taken in the fields near where I lived in Leyland. I'm wearing a black satin swimsuit with a white trim. The other was taken later the same year at the open-air swimming pool in Southport. I'm wearing a lemon and white checked bikini, bought for me by my boyfriend. It was the first time I had worn it and I felt like a film star. My feeling of conceit was short lived though, because when I jumped in the pool the shoulder strap broke and I had to scuttle out quickly feeling very embarrassed.

**Edna Lydiate, Preston**

## Recipe of the week

### Low–fat raspberry rice crumbles

**Serves 4**

- ◆ 6 low fat digestive biscuits
- ◆ 2 tsp ground ginger
- ◆ 2 tsp ground cinnamon
- ◆ 425g (17 oz) can of low–fat rice pudding
- ◆ 300g (12 oz) can of raspberries in fruit juice, drained
- ◆ 1 vanilla pod
- ◆ 1 tbsp honey

1. Preheat the oven to 200°C/400°F/Gas Mark 6. In a mixing bowl, add the raspberries and honey and mix together until the fruit is evenly coated.
2. Place the biscuits, ginger and cinnamon into a plastic bag and crush into crumbs.
3. In another mixing bowl, blend the rice pudding with the vanilla pod seeds.
4. Place the raspberries in four ovenproof ramekin dishes, followed by the vanilla rice pudding and sprinkle the biscuit mixture on top. Bake for 5-7 minutes, or until fully warm through and serve immediately.

Recipe: Canned Food UK, www.cannedfood.co.uk

# The dress

**B**ack in 1963, on my lunch break, I spied an amazing dress in the Peter Robinson shop on the Strand. It was £6 and I battled with my conscience over whether I could afford it. Ten minutes later it was in my bag. I was full of joy, albeit with an empty purse. I wore the dress to a big celebrity party where I was a hostess for a music magazine. That evening I mingled with pop stars and celebrities, chatting with the likes of Billy Fury, Joe Brown, Marty Wilde, Russ Conway, Tony Dalli, Pete Murray and even Jackie Collins. I was complimented on my dress on a number of occasions!

After a year of office work I needed a change

Ann modelling her 46-year-old dress

and I landed a job as a professional cabaret dancer at Butlins. The dress, of course, came with me and on days off I enjoyed the attention it brought.

Finally I joined the Marie De Vere Dance Agency in Charing Cross Road in London as a professional dancer. I took the dress to Italy, Spain, Portugal and danced heady nights away all over the world. After I got married and had my children I carefully packed the dress away. But, not long ago I rediscovered it again. I even put it on with full Sixties make-up to show my daughter. I told her to squint a little, so she would have a vague idea of how I looked in my 20s – I'm over 65 now after all!

**Ann Miller Allan, Seaford**

## Plant profile

### Crocosmia

**Height: 50cm**
**Spread: 35cm**
**Conditions: Thrives in well-drained soil and sun or dappled shade.**
The blazing flowers of crocosmia will add real heat to your borders. They require little attention and bloom reliably every summer. Colours range from the palest yellow through every shade of orange to scarlet. The clumps increase quickly in size, so may need dividing in autumn. Replant immediately and share any spares with your neighbours. Widely available from garden centres.

## Health tip

### Go all Mediterranean

Hang onto holiday habits by eating a Mediterranean style diet. Fresh fish, fruit, vegetables, wholegrains and olive oil could help you to stay younger for longer say US researchers.

## Senior moment

I was browsing in a shop and found a toy I quite liked for my dogs but I couldn't see a price. I was just about to ask the assistant when it dawned on me, just in time, that I was in a £1 shop!

**Maureen Spink, Tyne and Wear**

## Fast fact

Mark Twain classic The Adventures of Tom Sawyer was the first novel ever to be written on a typewriter and published. The novel about the mischievous little boy Tom was published in 1876.

## Small talk

My daughter ,Yvonne, and grandson, Jack, aged three, were out shopping when he declared that he needed the toilet. My daughter said: "Okay, but it's upstairs," and started heading towards the lift. "No Mummy," Jack said, "I don't want to go up the lift, I want to go up the calculator." She laughed so much that she needed the toilet too!

**Barbara Johnson, Swansea**

## Fashion we wore

This picture of me and my friend Alma Consterdine (née Taylor) was taken some time in the 1940s. How do you like the shorts we're wearing? We were on holiday at Butlins, Skegness. We both worked for Colgate-Palmolive in Salford and this was our last 'fling' before we got married. Sadly, both our husbands have died but we still have very happy memories.

**Jean Garside (nee Taylor), Salford**

# Recipe of the week

## Cheats mushroom and spinach lasagne
### Serves 4

- ◆ 2 tbsp olive oil
- ◆ 180 g (7 oz) spinach leaves
- ◆ 2 cloves garlic, chopped
- ◆ 250 g (10 oz) pack chestnut mushrooms, sliced
- ◆ 400 g (16 oz) can of chopped tomatoes with basil
- ◆ 300 g (12 oz) pack fresh lasagne sheets
- ◆ 2 x 200ml (8 fl oz) tub half-fat crème fraîche
- ◆ 100 g (4 oz) mature cheddar cheese
- ◆ 1/2 tsp freshly grated nutmeg
- ◆ Salt and pepper

1. Preheat the oven to 180°C/350°F/Gas Mark 4 and grease a 1.4 litre (2½ pint) ovenproof dish. In a large frying pan, heat half the oil and add the spinach and half of the garlic. Cook for 1-2 minutes, or until the spinach wilts. Season well and set aside.
2. Heat the remaining oil, add the mushrooms and cook for 6-8 minutes, or until they brown. Stir in the remaining garlic and tomatoes before bringing to the boil. Simmer for 2 minutes, or until the mixture has reduced. Season to taste.
3. In a small mixing bowl, combine the crème fraîche with the spinach and nutmeg.
4. Place a layer of lasagne sheets on the base of the ovenproof dish, top with half the mushroom mix, and then add another layer of lasagne. Spoon a third of the crème fraîche mixture and sprinkle over 1/3 cheddar cheese. Repeat these layers once more. Place a final layer of lasagne and spread over the remaining crème fraîche and cheese.
5. Bake for 25-30 minutes, or until the lasagne is bubbling and golden brown. Leave to cool for 5 minutes before serving with fresh green salad and garlic bread.

Recipe: Mushroom Bureau, www.mushroom-uk.com

# Frogspawn fun

I was the eldest of three sisters and had three brothers older than myself. I was forever making up games and 'things to do' for my two younger sisters. At night I would get under my bedclothes and pretend to be a voice on a radio. Another game was called 'money grabbing'. I had a large handful of foreign coins given to me by one of my brothers, which fascinated me. My sisters and I would sit on top of the bed and one of us would throw all the coins up into the air. We'd all make a grab for them and whoever grabbed the most would then become the thrower. We loved the jingley-jangley sound the coins made.

In those days we weren't restricted how far we

Beryl aged about eight

ventured and I remember having fun in a wood yard. There was a long path with a gateway at both ends and a stack of neatly packed new timber planks. When it rained the smell from these was magical. On the opposite side was the occasional barrel of water. The excitement created by these barrels was that they were full of frogspawn and we loved to collect baby frogs from the ground near the barrels into jars. The stacks of wood also had their amusement for us, along with the occasional splinter in our fingers. I find it hard to decide whether children are happier today than we were. We filled our time making our own amusements and enjoyed life to the full.

**Beryl Lucy, Manchester**

## Plant profile

### Cosmos at rosanguineus

**Height: 90cm**
**Spread: 55cm**
**Conditions: Loves a sunny position in well-drained soil.**

A tender perennial, this plant is extremely popular because it produces velvety, chocolate-scented flowers all summer. Great in a container on the terrace, where you can enjoy its irresistible perfume. Lift the tubers once the frosts have knocked back the leaves and store in a cool, dry place. Plant up again in spring and move outside in late May.

## Health tip

### Plum time

Make the most of gorgeous plums by stewing them, making them into crumbles or pots of lovely jam. US researchers have discovered that they rival the blueberry in the health-boosting antioxidant stakes.

## Senior moment

I had taken the children to see their grandmother and she had cooked them a pizza. "I've sprinkled some origami on it," said Granny. I think she meant Oregano!

**Angela Higinbotham, Cheshire**

## Fast fact

Legendary James Dean made jeans internationally cool in the Fifties. Before then denim was a working class uniform worn for its durability. When Marilyn Monroe sported a pair of blue denims in the 1954 film River of No Return, jeans became a hit with women too.

## Small talk

A friend who is a police dog handler was going to his car containing the dog behind the grille. A small boy looking into the car said: "Is that a dog in there?" "Yes", said my friend. The boy replied: "What did he do?"

**Mrs M L Stone, Essex**

## Fashion we wore

**H**ere's a snap of me and Margaret, who was my mum's friend's daughter. We were on a beach holiday in Bridlington. I'm on the left in the dark red swimming costume and Margaret is on the right wearing yellow. The new costumes, made of Nylon, had just come out and my mum was one of the first to buy them at a department store in Newcastle called Farnons. I think it must have been warmer in those days – either that or we were hardier souls who didn't feel the cold.

**Jackie Todd, Gateshead**

## Recipe of the week

### Fig clafouti
Serves 6

- ◆ 2 tbsp butter, melted
- ◆ 9 fresh figs, halved
- ◆ 3 medium eggs
- ◆ 3 level tbsp plain flour
- ◆ Pinch of salt
- ◆ 3 level tbsp caster sugar
- ◆ 450 ml (¾ pint) Gold Top milk
- ◆ 1 tbsp rum (optional)
- ◆ 2 tbsp flaked almonds
- ◆ Icing sugar, for dusting

1. Preheat the oven to 200°C/400°F/Gas Mark 6. Lightly grease a large ovenproof dish with some of the melted butter. Arrange the figs, cut side up, in the dish. Place in the oven for 5 minutes, or until warm.
2. Meanwhile in a large mixing bowl, beat the eggs before sifting in the flour and salt to form a smooth batter. Mix in the sugar.
3. In a small saucepan, heat the milk until tepid, then gradually whisk it into the batter mixture. Add the rum, if using.
4. Pour the warm batter over the figs in the dish. Drizzle the rest of the butter on top and sprinkle with flaked almonds.
5. Bake for 25-30 minutes, or until slightly raised round the edges and just set in the middle. Dust with icing sugar and serve warm, with a dollop of fresh cream.

Gold Top milk, www.gold-top.co.uk

# I remember steam trains

## BY: MARION CLARKE

Travelling in the days of steam was such fun that it's no surprise that Thomas the Tank Engine is a firm favourite with today's children who have only ever known diesel and electric trains.

The sense of adventure began with the hustle and bustle of the station. After buying a ticket (first, second or third class), there was no problem in finding a willing porter to take your suitcase on his trolley. The excitement really began when you reached the platform where your train was waiting, already puffing steam as if eager to be under way.

A glimpse into the guard's van revealed all manner of items consigned to his care, mail bags, bikes, a dog on a lead or children who were travelling unaccompanied by adults.

Passengers stowed their suitcases overhead in what looked like hammocks of netted cord. Once settled, there was time to study the faded pictures over the seats – usually of popular seaside resorts

## A loud clackety–clack as the train raced along

or panoramic views of lakes and mountains, all destinations that could be reached by rail.

Looking impressive in his uniform, the guard dropped his flag, blew his whistle and you were on your way. The engine pulled slowly out of the station, past suburban back gardens, then built up speed until you were hurtling past towns and villages.

The noise was tremendous; a loud clackety-clack as the train raced along the tracks and an ear-piercing blast on the driver's whistle as it whooshed into long, dark tunnels. If the window was open, the carriage filled with acrid smelling smoke and there was a rush to haul it up by the leather strap. (To leave the train, the window had to be lowered so you could reach out and turn the brass handle that opened the door from the outside. Today's health and safety inspectors would not approve!)

The 'golden age' of travel, when the journey was just as big a thrill as reaching your destination.

A real treat was to have lunch or tea in the buffet car. The steward would walk the length of the train loudly announcing that the meal was about to be served. Passengers left their seats and lurched along the narrow, swaying corridors to the buffet car where the tables were laid with crisp white cloths and gleaming cutlery.

For grown-ups as well as children, there was something quite magical about enjoying a meal while speeding through the countryside, returning the friendly waves of people working in the fields.

# Quiz of the month

All these events took place in the month of August over the past 60 years, but can you arrange them in the order that they happened?

PIC: REX FEATURES

**F** The Irish hostage, Brian Keenan, has been released in Beirut by his Islamic kidnappers after more than four years in captivity.

**G** The heir to the throne, Princess Elizabeth, has given birth to a daughter, Princess Anne, at Clarence House in London.

**H** Rudolf Hess, Hilter's right-hand man at the start of World War II, has been found dead in the grounds of Spandau Prison.

**I** Police in Los Angeles are investigating allegations of child abuse made against singer Michael Jackson.

**J** Marilyn Monroe has been found dead at her Los Angeles home. The 36-year-old actress' body was discovered by two doctors who were called to her home by a concerned housekeeper.

**K** Lord Hutton, the judge investigating the death of weapons expert Dr David Kelly, has opened his inquiry.

**L** Intimate photographs of the Duchess of York and a Texan businessman, John Bryan, have been published in a tabloid newspaper.

**M** Elvis Presley, 42, was found dead in a bathroom at his mansion in Memphis, Tennessee.

**N** Controversial horse rider Harvey Smith has been stripped of his winnings and show jumping title for allegedly making a rude 'V-sign' gesture in the direction of the judges.

**O** Brighton will become the first major resort in Britain to officially set aside part of its seafront to nudists.

**P** At least 30 people died when the Marchioness – a pleasure cruiser packed with young party-goers – collided with a barge on the River Thames.

**A** Yasser Arafat, the leader of the Palestine Liberation Organisation (PLO) has been forced out of Lebanon following the Israeli invasion.

**B** Troops in East Germany have sealed the border between East and West Berlin, shutting off the escape route for thousands of refugees from the East.

**C** Thousands of shops throughout England and Wales have opened legally on a Sunday for the first time following a change in the trading laws.

**D** The Ugandan leader, Idi Amin, has ordered the expulsion of most of the country's 60,000 Asians who are not Ugandan citizens.

**E** The South African-born British athlete, Zola Budd, is the centre of controversy for tangling with top American runner, Mary Decker, during the women's 3,000m Olympic final.

News stories taken from http://news.bbc.co.uk/onthisday/

ANSWER: G) 1950, B) 1961, J) 1962, N) 1971, D) 1972, M) 1977, O) 1979, A) 1982, E) 1984, H) 1987, P) 1989, L) 1990, F) 1992, I) 1993, C) 1994, K) 2003

# September 2010

Wednesday
1

Thursday
2

Friday
3

Saturday
4

Sunday
5

Monday
6

Tuesday
7

Wednesday
8

Thursday
9

Friday
10

Saturday
11

Sunday
12

Monday
13

Tuesday
14

Wednesday
15

Thursday
16

Friday
17

Saturday
18

Sunday
19

Monday
20

Tuesday
21

Wednesday
22

| Thursday 23 | Monday 27 |
| Friday 24 | Tuesday 28 |
| Saturday 25 | Wednesday 29 |
| Sunday 26 | Thursday 30 |

*Poetry corner*

# A fortnightly friend

I thought I'd write a poem,
About my special friend,
Who always makes me happy,
On whom I've come to depend.

She's full of stories and travel,
Beauty and fashion, too,
All sorts of hints and nostalgia,
To stop me feeling blue.

She talks of cookery and competitions,
Stories about the stars,
The ones who act in films and plays,
Not Jupiter or Mars.

Then she tells of Find a Friend,
You can write to if you wish,
Someone you could get to know,
Maybe seal with a loving kiss.

So here's how you get to know her
Her friendship reigns supreme,
You'll find her in the pages,
Of our lovely Yours magazine.
**Cindy Hagger, Romford, Essex**

# School days

**A**s a child I went to St Andrew's junior school in Leicester. The school building was quite old and there were only outside toilets. These were right at the other end of the playground. There was a row of about eight toilets and along the front was a fence so no one could see you sitting on the loo. If it was raining you tried very hard not to have to go to the toilet, because not only did you get wet running across the playground but also the toilet roof leaked so you got wet sitting there as well. In all the classrooms we had a big cast iron stove that had a coke fire burning in it all winter. There was a big fireguard around it so no one got burned, but we all liked to get a chair near it if we could.

We used to have free milk at school, little bottles that held one third of a pint. In the winter it was sometimes frozen so the teacher would put the crate

Margaret and her older sister Pat.

beside the fire to thaw it out. We had to take it in turns to be the 'milk monitor'. This meant it was that person's job to put the straws in all the bottles and hand the milk out to everyone. You also had to make sure all the bottles were put back in the crate and the dirty straws were thrown away. If there was any milk left the milk monitor could have extra if they wanted – or choose who to give it to. I liked the milk in the winter when it was served cold, but not in the summer when it was luke-warm.

**Margaret Whiltshire, Leicester**

## Plant profile

### White Egret Orchid

**Height: 30cm**
**Spread: 15cm**
**Conditions: Thrives in moist soil and light shade.**

Produced on slender arching stems, the pearly white flowers of Habenaria radiata look like a flock of miniature birds in flight, hence its name. It occurs naturally among the rice fields of Japan and does best in this country when planted in a container of moist compost and placed on a windowsill, in a greenhouse or, if your garden's quite sheltered, on the terrace. It's widely available online from specialist growers such as www.dejager.co.uk

## Health tip

### Get spicy

Swap salt for herbs and spices – it's not only good for your blood pressure, it's great for your general health too. Garlic is thought to help lower cholesterol, sage can help with menopausal symptoms and ginger could help to boost circulation.

## Senior moment

I saw my two chickens sheltering under the hedge as it was raining. An hour later they were still there which was unusual so I went to check. Only to find it wasn't their red heads I could see – it was two red flowers. **Mrs Wooldridge, Kent**

## Fast fact

Relative to its size, the tongue is the strongest muscle in the body. We're born with more than 10,000 taste buds on our tongue. Until the beginning of this century it was thought our taste buds could only recognise four basic tastes; sweet, sour, salty and bitter, but more recently a fifth taste, 'Unami', has been added to the list.

## Small talk

My great grandson, Rhys, aged four, loves his food. When shopping with his mother he was allowed some sausage rolls, and as they were small he was allowed two. So going home eating them he said to his mother: "If this is Heaven don't wake me up."

**Mrs A Jelfs, Evesham**

## Fashion we wore

This is a photo of me and my dear friend, Joan, taken on the seafront at Scarborough in 1953. Joan is on the left eating a cone of shrimps – I don't like them, but she loved them. We're both wearing matching shorts, which we had made by hand as we hadn't got a sewing machine. Sadly Joan passed away a few years ago but I love taking out old photos and remembering the wonderful times we had together as teenagers in Whitley Bridge.

**Mavis Knowles (née Maplebeck), Huddersfield**

## Recipe of the week

### Warm mushroom and sweet potato salad
Serves 4

- 500 g (20 oz) sweet potatoes, peeled
- 250 g (10 oz) large flat mushrooms, sliced
- 1 red pepper, deseeded and cut into chunks
- 1 red onion, thinly sliced
- 2 unpeeled garlic cloves
- 3 tbsp pine nuts
- 2 tbsp olive oil
- Juice of 1 lemon
- ½ tsp Dijon mustard
- A pinch of sugar
- 100 g (4 oz) salad leaves
- Salt and pepper

1. Preheat the oven to 180°C/350°F/Gas Mark 4. Chop the sweet potatoes into evenly sized large chunks. Place in a large roasting tin and drizzle over half the oil. Roast for 10 minutes, or until just tender.
2. Add the mushrooms, pepper, onion, garlic and pine nuts. Toss well to coat evenly and season. Roast for a further 15-20 minutes, or until the sweet potato is tender.
3. Into a small mixing bowl, de-skin the garlic and crush to a pulp. Add the remaining oil, lemon juice, mustard and sugar to make a dressing. Season to taste.
4. Empty the salad leaves onto a large serving plate and top with the roasted vegetables. Drizzle over the dressing and serve warm with some crusty bread.

Recipe: Mushroom Bureau, www.mushroom-uk.com

# Fun at Butlins

The summer of 1958 will be one I will never forget. I was only seven, but I can remember every minute of it. My parents had begrudgingly agreed to accompany friends for a week at Butlins. On arrival grinning Redcoats, singing along to the Butlins band, welcomed us.

We quickly settled into our delightful chalet and headed out eager to explore. There was so much to see. Turning one corner we were met with a free funfair, the next a massive football field and even an outdoor swimming pool surrounded by energetic swimmers and Redcoats bellowing orders over loud speakers. Everyone smiled.

There were umpteen signposts and without the map, we would still be completely lost! Dad, ever the detective, actually opened a door on to what was obviously the Board Room and sat at the head of the

Enjoying an early morning cuppa at Butlins.

table – possibly in Billy Butlin's own seat. Mum was mortified and yanked him out of the room, afraid that we would all be clapped in irons if the great man himself appeared. There was never a dull moment. Redcoat entertainment provided laughter for all ages and I remember one of the favourite performers was Des O'Connor. The children thought he was wonderful, Mum thought he was good looking and Dad said he had a good voice. Little did we know that he would go on to be a world-class entertainer. We all had such a good time. Funnily enough I can't remember the journey home – maybe we all fell asleep!	**Carol Tapp, Darwen**

## Plant profile

### Amaryllis belladonna

**Height: 60cm**
**Spread: 10cm**
**Conditions: Loves light, well-drained soils in full sun.**

Few bulbs produce such an amazing display of flowers – the rose-pink blooms are a joy in late summer and even more eye-catching because they're produced before the leaves. Plant at the base of a sheltered, sunny wall or, if your garden's exposed, in a greenhouse. Available online from www.dejager.co.uk

## Health tip

### Green fingers

Getting your garden sorted is a great way to get your daily dose of exercise, according to US researchers. All that bending, stretching, digging and hoeing will give your body a full workout.

## Senior moment

After being advised by the electricity company that we would have no power from 9.30am to 4.30pm, I told my family that I planned to use the time to catch up on some ironing.

**Mrs N Race, Devon**

## Fast fact

Buckingham Palace suffered nine direct bomb hits during the Second World War. Today Buckingham Palace has 775 rooms. These include 19 State rooms, 52 Royal and guest bedrooms, 188 staff bedrooms, 92 offices and 78 bathrooms. There is also a chapel, post office, swimming pool, doctors' surgery and even a cinema.

## Small talk

My daughter-in-law was trying to find a better route for a day out. Her young daughter said: "Mummy, are you insulting that map again?"

**Mrs M Townsend, Middlesex**

## Fashion we wore

I just had to share this photo of me and my wife, Margaret, taken on the pier in Great Yarmouth in August 1951. I was in the RAF at the time and had a week's leave before setting off to Germany. We were married the previous year, but we classed this break as our honeymoon, because we'd only had a week when we got married. Margaret is wearing a grey skirt, white blouse, a very bright blue cardigan and white sandals.

**Ernest Rudd, Sheffield**

## Recipe of the week

### Spiced apple and pear crumble cake

**Serves 10-12**

For the cake:
- ◆ 385 g (13 oz) can of sliced apples, drained and sliced
- ◆ 410 g (16 oz) can of pear quarters, drained and sliced
- ◆ 180 g (7 oz) caster sugar
- ◆ 180 g (7 oz) butter, softened
- ◆ 150 g (6 oz) self-raising flour
- ◆ 50 g (2 oz) ground almonds
- ◆ 3 eggs
- ◆ 1-2 tbsp milk
- ◆ 1 tsp ground cinnamon

For the crumble:
- ◆ 50 g (2 oz) caster sugar
- ◆ 100 g (4 oz) butter
- ◆ 125 g (5 oz) self-raising flour
- ◆ 1 tsp ground cinnamon

1. Preheat the oven 180°C/ 350°F/Gas Mark 4. Grease and line the base of a 23 cm (9 in) round, deep cake tin. In a mixing bowl toss the fruit with half of the cinnamon and set aside.
2. For the crumble, take another mixing bowl and rub the butter into the flour with your fingertips, until it resembles fine breadcrumbs. Add the remaining cinnamon and sugar, mix well and set aside.
3. For the cake, in a large mixing bowl beat together the butter and sugar until pale. Add the remaining ingredients and mix until combined. Pour into the cake tin, place the fruit on the top and sprinkle with the crumble mixture.
4. Bake for 50-55 minutes, or until firm and golden. Leave to cool slightly on a wire rack before serving with a generous helping of creamy custard or ice cream.

Recipe: Canned Food UK, www.cannedfood.co.uk

# Cosy by the fireside

I'm a miner's daughter, so I was brought up with memories of a welcoming coal fire. It was a large black fireplace with an oven at the side of it, just like the fireplaces you see at Beamish Museum. We used to have a fender around the fireplace with small soft seats on either end of it.

I still remember sitting on one, while my brother sat on the other, gazing into the flames and seeing different pictures – we were easily amused! I was allowed to tear pieces of paper into smaller pieces and throw them onto the flames. The flames would then dart upwards – smoke swirling up the chimney.

The highlight was when we were allowed to put coal on the fire. We were fascinated as the fire

Audrey and her brother George in 1949 and their dog Silver

darkened and then quickly the flames started to brighten and lick around the new coal.

We were very lucky to have two fireplaces in our home. Every day the living room fire warmed the house. However, the fire in the front room, our best room, was only lit on Sundays. When we came home from Sunday School my brother and I used to peep through the window to make sure that the fire was still there to welcome us home. It was always hot buttered toast for tea. We were allowed to toast our own bread, which was held on an old metal toasting fork over the open fire. I still remember the delicious smell of the toast that used to fill the house with warmth.

**Audrey Faul (née Maidment), Hartlepool**

## Plant profile

### Echinacea purpurea

**Height: 70cm**

**Spread: 35cm**

**Conditions: Loves a well-drained soil in full sun or partial shade but will also cope on heavy soils.**

Commonly known as the purple coneflower and often used medicinally, this variety of echinacea produces large daisy–like flowers with lavender petals around a red pincushion-like centre. Echinaceas are great in summer borders with a vigorous, upright, branching habit and a long flowering period. Widely available from garden centres.

## Health tip

### Milk it

Skimmed milk and low-fat dairy products could help to lower your blood pressure says research by the Dairy Council. Dairy foods provide minerals such as calcium and potassium which are important for regulating your blood pressure.

## Senior moment

A friend came round for coffee and was telling me some news but I couldn't hear her clearly. Without thinking, I picked up the remote control, pointed it towards her and pressed the volume button!

**Berry Welster, Birmingham**

## Fast fact

Big Ben celebrated its 150th anniversary in 2009. The clock itself started May 31, 1859 and the great bell's chimes were first heard on July 11 of that year. The clock tower at the north-eastern end of the Palace of Westminster is the world's largest four-faced chiming clock. It is also the third-tallest free-standing clock tower in the world.

## Small talk

During a recent holiday in America, my ten-year-old daughter and I visited New York. I told her that it was the city that never sleeps. After a moment's thought, she replied: "I'm not surprised, there is a coffee shop on every corner."

**Frances Bourne, Birmingham**

## Fashion we wore

I love this old photo of me with blonde hair and a 21-inch waist. I must have been about 20 years old because it was taken in 1961. I'm wearing a lilac Crimplene suit with a crisp white cotton blouse – I must have taken the jacket off because it was such a hot sunny day. Of course my pointed high-heeled shoes were also white to match my handbag. The other people in the photo are my friend Winifred and her boyfriend David Walton. We had just returned from a mutual friend's wedding. My boyfriend, Don, took the photo and later became my husband of 34 years.

**Audrey Faul, Hartlepool**

## Recipe of the week

### Chicken and tomato crumble
Serves 4

- ◆ 2 tbsp Rapeseed oil
- ◆ 400 g (16 oz) chicken breast, diced
- ◆ 200 g (8 oz) frozen peas
- ◆ 200 g (8 oz) can of sweetcorn, drained
- ◆ 700 g (1 lb 8 oz) jar tomato pasta sauce
- ◆ 25 g (1 oz) oats
- ◆ 150 g (6 oz) wholemeal breadcrumbs

1. Preheat the grill to a medium to high heat. In a large frying pan, heat the oil and fry the chicken for 4-5 minutes. Add the vegetables and cook for a further 1-2 minutes.
2. Stir in the pasta sauce, bring to the boil and simmer for 2-3 minutes, or until the chicken is fully cooked. Transfer to an ovenproof serving dish.
3. In a small mixing bowl, combine the oats and breadcrumbs and sprinkle over the chicken. Place under the grill for 4-5 minutes, or until the top is golden brown and the chicken mix is bubbling. Leave to cool slightly before serving with brown rice or a fresh salad.

Recipe: Rapeseed Oil, www.hgca.com

# The Baedeker Raids

For me living in Coulsdon, near Croydon during the war was not as frightening as you might think. My father, however, who worked at Bricklayers Arms engine depot not far from Waterloo station, didn't have a pleasant time commuting daily into London. In 1942 he welcomed a transfer to the quiet market town of Exeter. We'd only been there a couple of months when German bombers came in low and dropped a few bombs. The attack on Exeter on the night of April 23, took everyone by surprise. It was the first of what became known as the 'Baedeker Raids'.

The Lutwaffe selected cities, which had three stars in the Baedeker tourist guide. The bombers came back the following night but there was little damage and we thought that would be the end. But,

Air Rangers marching in front of the bank with its missing roof

on May 4, we heard the air-raid sirens once more and we knew at once that this was going to be different. There was the ominous thump, thump, thump of German bombers as more and more of them arrived overhead. Flares lit up the sky as the planes approached their target.

Soon incendiary bombs rained down on the town, and the white light of the flares was replaced by the red glow of buildings on fire – devastating the town.

When I later joined the Air Rangers the local press photographed us parading down the High Street. At the time it didn't seem at all odd that the bank had its roof missing.

**Maureen Lamb, Cumbria**

## Plant profile

### Polianthes tuberosa 'The Pearl'

**Height: 90cm**
**Spread: 10cm**
**Conditions: Thrives in a light, well-drained soil and a sunny position.**
Producing spires of highly fragrant, waxy, semi–double white flowers during late summer, it's an excellent container plant. Imagine it scenting the breeze at sunset, while you relax with a glass of something special! Unsurprisingly, it's popular in flower arrangements and is used in the production of cologne around the world. Available online from specialist suppliers including www.vanmeuwen.com

## Health tip
### Let it all out

US Brits are the angriest nation in Europe, but we're the least likely to show our frustration says research by the British Association of Anger Management. Bottling up your rage isn't good for your health – so voice your frustrations every now and again. Visit www.angermanage.co.uk for advice.

## Senior moment

Having a cup of tea in a café, I spilled some and wiped it up with a serviette. Seeing a stainless steel bin I put the serviette in. "Have you just put something in that bin?" a voice said. "Yes," I replied. The voice said: "That's my bin, I've just bought it."

**Valerie Griffee, Bristol**

## Fast fact

Contrary to popular belief the classic 1973 Hovis advert featuring the small boy pushing his bike up a hill was not filmed in the North of England, but on Gold Hill in Shaftesbury, Dorset. The commercial was directed by Ridley Scott – better known for the Alien and Gladiator films.

## Small talk

My small grandson was showing me how well he could ride his new bike. "That's very good," I said, "I couldn't ride like that when I was five." Sam replied, "No, you couldn't grandma because bikes hadn't been invented when you were little."

**Mrs E Morley, Thirsk**

## Fashion we wore

**H**ere are a couple of photos of my friend Anne and I taken in the early Fifties. In the first Anne is on the right. Our tiered skirts were really fashionable at the time – mine was blue and white striped, while Anne's had a black and white floral pattern. I'm also wearing sheer nylon gloves, which were a must-have item. All our clothes in those days came from C&A in Croydon. In the other photo we had raided my mother's wardrobe and tried on all her clothes while she was working.

**Patricia Franklin, Ayrshire**

## Recipe of the week

### Fat-free fruit tea loaf
**Makes: 10-12 Slices**

- 1 x Darjeeling tea bag
- 300 g (12 oz) soft dried fruit, (apricots, prunes, apples etc), roughly chopped
- 175 g (7 oz) soft brown sugar
- 2 medium eggs, beaten
- 225 g (9 oz) wholemeal flour
- 1 tsp baking powder
- 1 tsp mixed spice

1. Grease and line the base of a 1 kg (2 lb 2 oz) loaf tin.
2. In a large mixing bowl, soak the tea bag in 300 ml (12 fl oz) boiling water for 5 minutes. Discard the tea bag before adding the fruit and soak for 2-3 hours.
3. Meanwhile, preheat the oven to 180C/350°F/ Gas Mark 4.
4. In another mixing bowl, combine the sugar and eggs. Mix in the flour, baking powder and mixed spice and fold into the fruit mixture.
5. Pour into the prepared tin and bake for 1½ hours, or until firm to the touch and a skewer comes out clean. Transfer to a wire rack and allow to cool before slicing.

Recipe: Wholegrain Goodness, www.wholegraingoodness.com

# Mini and me

In 1959 the Mini was born, and funnily enough so was I. So, Mini and I have grown up together. I bought my first Mini from my uncle when I was 18. I hand painted it daffodil yellow with purple stripes and discovered you can fit a whole badminton team in a Mini. My second Mini was black and classy. Purchased with the proceeds of my divorce, it heralded a new start for me.

Stolen from a hospital car park on my (and Mini's) 30th birthday, the police officer looked totally bemused as I whimpered: "And it's our birthdays!"

Millie was my 40th birthday present, a 40th anniversary limited edition, she drew attention wherever we went. No quick dash to the supermarket in Millie, people young and old constantly accosted me. Invariably their opening

Alison standing proudly alongside her beloved Mini.

words were, 'I remember my Mini'. Millie brought pleasure to everyone.

She stayed with me for eight years but eventually I decided it was time to sell. Millie was no longer coping with modern day roads and speed bumps were a real problem, we had to stop and crawl over each one. My husband had to do the deal, I was a simpering wreck as I said goodbye to my beloved little car.

Mini and I have had some great birthday celebrations and I have been to Mini's 30th, 40th and now 50th parties. I fully intend to be at the 60th, this time perhaps in a modern Mini, growing old together.

**Alison Sadler, Sheffield**

## Plant profile

### Colchicums

**Height: 8cm**
**Spread: 9cm**
**Conditions: Plant 15cm deep in well-drained soil in sun or shade.**

Producing crocus-shaped pink blooms well before the leaves, these charming plants make quite a statement during the autumn months. This lack of foliage has led to them being given the saucy name of naked ladies. One of their greatest attributes is their ability to grow in shade, so try planting them beneath trees to brighten the gloom. They're widely available as bulbs from garden centres in late summer.

## Health tip
### Sleep away senior moments

If your memory leaves a lot to be desired get some sleep. US scientists have discovered that sleep helps you to consolidate memories and gives your brain a chance to reorganise what you've learnt that day.

## Senior moment

I couldn't find my glasses, but went ahead and began applying my make up. I was popping on a slick of lip gloss, when my lips started to feel a bit stiff and I noticed a funny smell. I had used nail varnish instead of lip gloss! I don't think it's a look that will catch on.
**Gloria Sewell, Kent**

# Fast fact

Although Audrey Hepburn was nominated for an Academy Award for her role in Breakfast At Tiffany's she didn't win. Author Truman Capote was also said to be unhappy with the final film and even claimed he would have preferred Holly Golightly to be played by Marilyn Monroe.

# Small talk

Chatting with my grandson Elliott, aged six, I asked him what he liked most about his recent holiday in Tenerife. He furrowed his brow, then replied that he liked the sun. I had expected him to say the beach or swimming pool. It goes to show that little things mean a lot. **Mrs S M Foster, East Yorkshire**

# Fashion we wore

I thought readers might like to see this picture that I took of my friend Pat Digby (née Mills), on holiday in Jersey. It was 1958 and as you can see fancy petticoats were all the rage. Pat's 'perma-pleated' cotton skirt was turquoise. The underskirt had five or six layers, each bound with pastel coloured bias binding. Our holiday was great fun and Pat was thrilled to fly for the first time. She was really disappointed when we had to return by boat because there was too much fog for the plane to take off.

**Jill Edwards, Walthamstow**

## Butternut squash and bean casserole

Serves 4

- ◆ 1 medium butternut squash, cut into 2.5 cm chunks
- ◆ 12 shallots, peeled and left whole
- ◆ 6 sage leaves, roughly chopped
- ◆ 3 tbsp extra virgin olive oil
- ◆ 3 cloves garlic, crushed
- ◆ 1 tbsp flour
- ◆ 175 ml (7 fl oz) white wine
- ◆ 400 g (16 oz) can of butterbeans, drained and rinsed
- ◆ 400 ml (16 fl oz) vegetable stock
- ◆ 2 tbsp sun-dried tomato paste

For the dumplings:
- ◆ 200 g (8 oz) self-raising flour
- ◆ 100 g (4 oz) vegetable suet
- ◆ 2 tsp dried mixed herbs
- ◆ Salt and black pepper
- ◆ 5-8 tbsp cold water

1. Preheat the oven to 200°C/400°F/Gas Mark 6. Roast the butternut squash and shallots with the oil and sage leaves for 20-30 minutes, or until the vegetables are browned. Season well.
2. Meanwhile, make the dumplings in a large mixing bowl. Combine all the dry ingredients and add enough cold water to form a soft dough. Shape into 8 small balls and set aside.
3. Turn down the oven to 180°C/350°F/Gas Mark 4. Coat the vegetables in the flour, before adding the white wine, scraping the bottom to release all the sticky caramelised residue.
4. Transfer to an ovenproof casserole dish and add the beans, tomato paste and enough stock to cover the vegetables. Stir well; bring to the boil and cover. Cook in the oven for 30 minutes.
5. Then gently add the dumpling and return to the oven uncovered for 20 minutes, or until the dumplings are crispy on the outside and fluffy and cooked through on the inside.
6. Serve immediately with mashed potato and green beans . Recipe: UK Shallots, www.ukshallot.com

# I remember The Famous Five

BY: MARION CLARKE

Long before Harry Potter was a twinkle in the eye of J K Rowling, children saved their pocket money to buy the latest Famous Five adventure by Enid Blyton. It was a joyful day when you had accrued enough sixpences to go to the bookshop and purchase your very own hardback edition of Five Go to Smuggler's Top or Five Go Off in a Caravan.

Once you had bought it, you could hardly wait to curl up in chair and catch up on the latest escapades of Julian, Dick and Anne, their cousin George, and George's dog, Timmy. Long after you'd been told to turn off the bedside lamp, you'd still be reading with your torch hidden under the blanket.

George, as all fans know, was really a girl (Georgina) who looked and behaved like a boy. Enid Blyton claimed to have based the character on herself as a child. Anne could hardly have been more different – she had a strong domestic bent (preparing the food and doing the washing up when the children go camping) and was really very nervous of the gang's tendency to find themselves in dangerous situations.

## Julian, the eldest, was naturally the leader

Julian, the eldest, was naturally the leader and rather bossy while Dick was dependable, kind and funny.

Most of the adventures took place in the school holidays when Julian, Dick and Anne go to Cornwall where George's parents (Uncle Quentin and Aunt Fanny) have their home and are also the owners of Kirrin Island. Imagine the thrill of owning your very own island!

The children were admirably independent, roaming the countryside on their bikes and whatever danger they found themselves in – often involving criminal gangs, hidden caves and secret tunnels – they solved the problem without the help of grown-ups. But what would they have done without Timmy, a mongrel of remarkable intelligence who rounds up the baddies and even trots off to the police station to alert the CID? George, quite rightly, thinks he is the best dog in the world.

**FIVE ON A TREASURE ISLAND**

*Enid Blyton*

H&S

PIC: ALAMY

Adventure and escapism awaited inside each book.

In 1957 the film Five on a Treasure Island was released and in the 1970s a television series brought the adventures of the Five to another generation of children – but nothing could compare with the excitement of flipping over the pages of those precious first editions.

Enid Blyton planned to write only six or eight books featuring the Famous Five but, luckily for her young readers, they proved so successful that she went on to write 21. A prolific writer, she churned out 10,000 words a day at her home, Green Hedges in Beaconsfield. Blyton once responded to criticism of her books by saying that she paid no attention to the comments of anyone over the age of 12. Thank goodness for that!

# Quiz of the month

All these events took place in the month of September over the past 60 years, but can you arrange them in the order that they happened?

PIC: REX FEATURES

**A** A massive Russian rocket, Lunik II, has been successfully launched at the Moon carrying 86olb (391kg) of scientific instruments.

**B** A report sponsored by the government has suggested homosexual behaviour between consenting adults should no longer be a criminal offence.

**C** A two-tier postal system begins with the introduction of first and second class stamps.

**D** Bulgarian dissident Georgi Markov has died, four days after being stabbed with an umbrella at a London bus stop.

**E** David Mellor has resigned as heritage minister, blaming his departure on a constant barrage of hostile stories in the tabloid press following the disclosure of his affair with the actress Antonia de Sancha.

**F** English cricket captain Graham Gooch and seven other members of his squad have been refused visas to travel to India.

**G** Guitarist Jimi Hendrix has died after collapsing at a party in London.

**H** More than 6o million Americans tuned in to watch the first ever televised debate between presidential candidates – Richard Nixon and John F Kennedy.

**I** Police have discovered the body of a young woman – thought to be the 12th victim of the 'Yorkshire Ripper'.

**J** The Hollywood film star James Dean (24) has been killed in a road accident in California, USA.

**K** The Queen has officially opened Europe's longest suspension bridge linking Edinburgh to Perth across the River Forth.

**L** The United States and the USSR are to sign an agreement to reduce the number of nuclear missiles held by the superpowers over the next few years.

**M** Thirty-eight Republican inmates have escaped from a high-security Maze prison in Northern Ireland.

**N** Three weeks of border clashes between Iran and Iraq appear to have finally erupted into all-out war.

**O** Two people were killed and 63 injured when a suspected IRA bomb exploded in the lobby of the Hilton hotel in central London.

**P** Yitzhak Rabin, the Israeli prime minister and Yasser Arafat the leader of the Palestine Liberation Organisation have signed a deal giving Palestinians control over much of the West Bank.

News stories taken from http://news.bbc.co.uk/onthisday/

ANSWER: J) 1955, B) 1957, A) 1959, H) 1960, K) 1964, C) 1968, G) 1970, O) 1975, D) 1978, I) 1979, N) 1980, M) 1983, L) 1987, F) 1988, E) 1992, P) 1995

# Curtain up!

BY: VERONICA RYDER

## Ellen shuns the limelight – until the day she has to save the show

**S**ilence. I repeated the line, louder: "I knew what I'd done as soon as the door closed."

"I'm sorry, dear," Mildred's voice floated over from stage left. "I thought we were on the bit where I ask Tim what he was doing in the garden."

"Right! That's it, cast. I cannot take any more of this." Brian, our director, was about to throw a wobbly. "Everyone on stage, please."

I wasn't sure if 'everyone' included me, the prompt, but I sidled round the edge of the stage anyway. To my horror, Brian came over and took my elbow, leading me out in front of the cast.

He said: "You all know Ellen. She plays a vital part but it is supposed to be a non-speaking one. This afternoon I have heard Ellen's voice FAR TOO MUCH. More than I have heard your voice, Mildred. Why do you think that is?"

Mildred turned bright red and her bottom lip quivered. She said nothing.

"Still no word from our leading lady?" Brian enquired acidly. "Perhaps, she cannot speak without a prompt. Perhaps, she will never say another word unless Ellen says it first."

He released my arm and I edged back to the side

## 'I have heard Ellen's voice far too much.'

of the stage. I was not used to being in the limelight.

Brian continued: "I suggest we call it a day, and reflect on how we can improve things before the next rehearsal. Remember, it will be you looking foolish up there in front of the audience, not me. See you tomorrow – seven o'clock prompt."

No one suggested a quick one in the Turk's Head. Things were as bad as they could be – or so I thought.

Next evening, I arrived to find Brian pacing the stage. One pair of glasses dangled on a cord round his neck, another pair perched on top of his head. His looked as if he hadn't slept for a week.

"She's pulled out, the old bat," he announced.

"Who?" I asked.

"Mildred. She rang me this morning and said I'd humiliated her in front of everyone and she was too upset to carry on. Upset!" The pacing continued. "I'll give her upset! What about the show? What about the rest of the team? What about me?"

"Did you try and persuade her?" I asked.

"I told her to take a running jump, actually," Brian replied. "I can't be doing with these amateur prima donnas."

**T**he rest of the cast had arrived and Brian announced the bad news. I watched their faces register shock. They say there is often more drama offstage than on – and this was one of those times.

"We'll have to cancel," Jocelyn said, tearfully.

"Cancel be damned," retorted Geoffrey. "The show must go on."

Brian agreed: "No one is indispensable. Who is Mildred's understudy?"

Thelma put her hand up.

"You? But you're playing Arabella – how come you're understudying the lead?"

"If you remember, I auditioned for the lead but Mildred got it – I expect you were being kind."

"Kind?" Brian looked horrified, as if Thelma had accused him of some kind of perversion. "Okay, so who's your understudy then?"

"Angela."

"So, let's phone Angela."

"Um, we can't do that," I advised nervously.

"Why not? Here's my mobile."

"No, I mean we can't because she's on holiday. In Patagonia."

There was an ominous silence. Then Brian let rip.

"So we can't do the show because the one person we need is prancing around in flipping Patagonia. For heaven's sake, save me from amateur productions!"

He turned to me. "Make a note, Ellen. I will NEVER work with this company again."

As he said this before every show and at various

# He was still looking at me, a strange light in his eye

stages of rehearsals, the reaction was muted, but I made a note anyway. When I glanced up, he was still looking at me, a strange light in his eye.

"You, Ellen – you can do it. You can save the show, be our Daphne. You know the words."

I tried to say I couldn't possibly; I was strictly a backstage person, not a performer. But the rest of the cast joined in.

"You can do it, Ellen."

"You'll be brilliant."

With a flourish, Brian went down on one knee.

"Darling Ellen, will you do me the honour of becoming my Daphne?"

Somehow 'I couldn't possibly' became 'I will' and the whole cast cheered. I felt a warm glow, though the moment was marred by Gerald saying: "Anyway, Daphne's dead by the end of Scene Two, so then we get our prompt back."

"There's one condition," I said.

Brian looked wary: "You can't have your own dressing room."

"No, it's Daphne's outburst – I just couldn't say the swear word she uses."

There was a stunned silence at this new setback.

Brian put his arm round me. "But it won't be Ellen out there, will it? It will be nasty Daphne who riles people so much that someone wants to kill her. Think of it as a challenge, sweetie."

He kissed me on the cheek, then said briskly: "Right, back to work everyone – from the top."

And so, with a lot of makeup and soft lighting, I became Daphne and made my acting (and swearing) debut. I'd like to report that an agent spotted my talent and whisked me off to the West End but this is not a fairy story.

Mildred has since returned to the company so what they really need is a reliable prompt!

# October 2010

Friday
1

Saturday
2

Sunday
3

Monday
4

Tuesday
5

Wednesday
6

Thursday
7

Friday
8

Saturday
9

Sunday
10

Monday
11

Tuesday
12

Wednesday
13

Thursday
14

Friday
15

Saturday
16

Sunday
17

Monday
18

Tuesday
19

Wednesday
20

Thursday
21

Friday
22

| | |
|---|---|
| **Saturday**<br>23 | **Thursday**<br>28 |
| **Sunday**<br>24 | **Friday**<br>29 |
| **Monday**<br>25 | **Saturday**<br>30 |
| **Tuesday**<br>26 | **Sunday**<br>31<br>Hallowe'en<br>British Summer Time ends |
| **Wednesday**<br>27 | |

PIC: REX FEATURES

## Poetry corner

# Teen dreams

I once wore high heels,
But now it's flat shoes,
I once let out squeals,
When Tommy sang the blues.

I once rock 'n' rolled,
Until the late hour,
But now I'm too old,
With no staying-power.

I once wore dresses,
With layers of net,
And my long tresses,
Were loose and not set.
My hair that had style,

Is grey and like straw,
My tights are thick lyle,
Not sheer anymore.

My teeth were all mine,
They were strong and white,
But like stars that shine,
Now come out at night.
Once I was skinny,

Proud of my figure,
Now my old pinny,
Hides hips much bigger.

But, oh what the heck,
What will be will be,
I may be an old wreck,
But I'm happy with me.
**Renne Dunbar, Derbyshire**

# Fond Butlins memories

**Gail in her Butlins Redcoat**

**A**s a student in the Sixties I needed some extra money, so I applied to Butlins to work as a Redcoat. Weeks after my interview I got a letter saying I had been accepted and that I would be working at the Pwellhi Camp in North Wales. Along with the letter came a list of my duties, what was expected of a Butlins Redcoat and dress requirements. In my case there were two pairs of white high-heels and white tennis shoes. To go with my Redcoat uniform I had two pairs of shorts for the games that were held each week. I also had a bathing costume and 'mufti' for my one day off.

The day came and with more than a little nervousness I made my way to Chesterfield railway station. The train pulled into the camp and after getting off I found my way to the Entertainments Office where I met the manager and some of the Redcoat team. I was then taken to the uniform centre and given two red blazers, two white pleated skirts and three blouses.

My first few days were very difficult and I wondered if I'd done the right thing. But, once settled in I loved every minute. I was quite athletic in those days and at school had done trampolining, so I did this on the sports field. And, like all the others, I had to perform each night in the Redcoat show. Even now I can remember the steps of the dance that we did at the beginning of the show.

**Gail Storey, Derbyshire**

## Plant profile

### Anemone 'Hadspen Abundance'

**Height: 50cm**
**Spread: 35cm**
**Conditions: Thrives in moist soil and partial shade.**

Japanese anemones are an elegant addition to any garden, producing pretty flowers on airy stems from August onwards. Perfect for the back of a border with flowers ranging in colour from white through every shade of pink to purple. This variety produces attractive purple flowers on a compact plant. The contrast between the purple petals and the golden anthers is magical. Widely available with many varieties having an RHS Award of Garden Merit.

## Health tip

### What did you say?

Check your hearing by calling the RNID's telephone hearing check 0844 800 3838 (calls from a BT landline cost up to 5p per minute. Other providers' charges may vary. Call set up charge may apply). Or do it online at www.rnid.org.uk.

## Senior moment

I noticed my husband fiddling with his personal stereo cassette player, muttering under his breath that he couldn't hear any music. I looked across and calmly suggested that if he plugged the headphones back in it might cure the problem.

**Barbara Gray, East Yorks**

## Fast fact

The London premiere of the first Bond film Dr No was held at the London Pavilion on October 5, 1962. The title role was taken by our favourite 007 – Sean Connery – who went on to star in another seven Bond classics. The Scot has even expressed an interest in playing a future Bond villain – watch this space.

## Small talk

It was a very cold morning as my children went to school so I decided to make a warming homemade soup. When they came home I proudly placed a bowl of steaming soup in front of them. As I walked away, I heard my son say to my daughter: "Why can't we have proper soup out of a tin?"  **Mrs S Lever, Wilts**

## Fashion we wore

This photo is of me and my future husband at Butlins Holiday Camp, Skegness. It was taken in 1948 and we were married the following year. I'm wearing a pink dress from C&A, a navy cardigan and navy and white, two-tone shoes. My husband is wearing; a brown check sports jacket, dark grey striped 'flannels' and a Fair Isle pullover which had been hand-knitted for him by his aunt.

**Marion Bennett, Leicester**

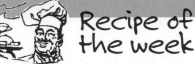

# Recipe of the week

PIC: STEVE BAXTER

## Rum and raisin custards
**Makes 6**

- ◆ 85 g (3oz) raisins
- ◆ 3 tbsp dark rum
- ◆ ½ tsp nutmeg
- ◆ 284 ml (11 oz) carton whipping cream
- ◆ 100 ml (4 fl oz) semi-skimmed milk
- ◆ 4 large egg yolks
- ◆ 6 tbsp Carnation condensed milk
- ◆ Caster sugar, to glaze

1. Soak the raisins in the rum for an hour or overnight.
2. Preheat the oven to 150°C/300°F/Gas Mark 2. Divide the raisins between six ramekins or similar sized coffee cups.
3. In a medium saucepan, combine the cream, milk and nutmeg and gently bring to the boil. In a jug, mix the egg yolks and condensed milk before gradually pouring the cream mixture onto the eggs, stirring continuously to combine.
4. Divide the custard mixture into the ramekins.
5. Place them in a deep baking tin and fill the tin with enough boiling water to come halfway up the sides of the dishes. Cover with foil and bake for 40 minutes, or until just set and wobbly in the middle.
6. Place on a wire rack to cool before chilling well.
7. To glaze: preheat the grill to high. Sprinkle a thin layer of caster sugar over each dish, ensuring the custard is covered. Grill for 5-6 minutes, or until the sugar has melted to golden brown. This stage needs constant observation. Cool slightly before serving.

Recipe: Nestlé Carnation, www.carnation.co.uk

## All in our stride

I was 14 when war was declared. I had embarked on a two-year domestic science course on the outskirts of London where air-raids were frequent.

Following school I trained as a nursery nurse and also did a spell working at a children's hospital. When I was 18 I worked as a Staff Nurse and later a Deputy Matron at local day nurseries. One of the nurseries catered for mothers who worked night shifts at the Woolwich Arsenal munitions factory. Out of the 50 children, aged five years and under, that we looked after, half stayed at night. Babies were tucked up in cots and toddlers on stretcher beds with two sleeping staff and one on duty. At the sound of the siren sleeping staff were alerted

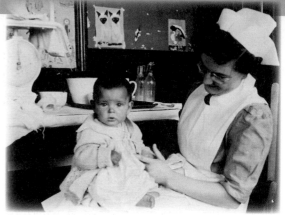

Jean working as a nursery nurse during the war.

and babies and toddlers would be carried, complete with mattresses, to the shelter. The procedure would often be carried out several times a night, only on very bad nights were we allowed to leave the children in the shelters – and never alone. Like many people during the war our nights were spent sleeping in public and private underground shelters. Whole neighbourhoods disappearing underground with bundles of bedding became a common sight. It was hair-raising at times, but young and old alike learned to take it in their stride.

**Jean Greenslade, Devon**

## Plant profile

### Schizostylis coccinea

**Height: 50cm**
**Spread: 15cm**
**Conditions: Thrives in dry, light, sandy soils and a sunny position.**

Elegant in habit, the Kaffir Lily, as it's commonly known, flowers prettily in late summer, adding a welcome splash of colour to the garden. Several popular varieties are available with blooms ranging in colour from white through every shade of pink to red. It looks most effective when grown in small clumps. Widely available from garden centres, it has an Award of Garden Merit from the RHS.

## Health tip
### Veg out

The secret to staying bug-free this winter is to fill your diet with fruit and veg. The more antioxidant rich veggies you eat the lower your risk of catching a cold say Australian dieticians.

## Senior moment

We like to go to our local club to play bingo. I was busy reading one day when my husband remarked: "The bingo's out tomorrow." "There's no bingo tomorrow," I corrected him. Very amused, he replied: "No, the bin goes out tomorrow."

**Mrs B Stebbings, Crewe**

## Fast fact

The first modern bra to receive a patent was one invented by New York socialite, Mary Phelps Jacob, in 1914. Apparently the previous year she had bought a sheer evening gown for a social event and found the corset she would usually have worn as an undergarment was visible around the plunging neckline. Two silk handkerchiefs and some pink ribbon later the bra was born.

## Small talk

Ollie, my young grandson, loves living in their Victorian four-storey house. So when he heard his parents discussing the possibility of moving, he got quite upset. He told them: "I can't go, because I've lost my ball in the garden."

**Joyce Mansell, Cheshire**

## Fashion we wore

This picture was taken in 1952 in Dublin, Ireland. I was 19 at the time and rock 'n' roll was all the rage. My skirt was made of pink felt material and I cut the letters 'Elvis Presley' and the outline of a guitar out of black felt and sewed them on. Under the skirt were layers of stiff petticoats, which made the skirt stick out. I also wore a black 'Waspie' belt and a blouse in a deeper shade of pink. I loved this outfit because it was one-of-a-kind and I knew when I wore it to a dance I wouldn't see anyone wearing anything quite like it.

**Christina Kelly, Worcester**

## Recipe of the week

### Quick fish pie

**Serves 4**

- 750 g (1 lb 8 oz) King Edward potatoes, cut into large chunks,
- 25 g (1 oz) butter
- 3 tbsp milk
- 350 g (14 oz) salmon, cubed,
- 250 g (10 oz) cod fillet, cubed,
- 100 g (4 oz) peas
- 200 g (8 oz) crème fraîche
- Salt and pepper

1. Preheat the oven to 200C/400°F/Gas Mark 6. In a large saucepan, boil the potatoes for 10-12 minutes, or until tender. Drain and mash with the butter and milk. Season to taste.
2. In a saucepan of boiling water, cook the fish for 5 minutes. Drain and return to the pan. Add the peas, crème fraîche and cook gently for 2-3 minutes. Season to taste.
3. Transfer to an ovenproof dish and top with the mashed potato. Bake for 10 minutes, or until the top is golden brown and crispy.

Recipe: Love Potatoes, www.britishpotatoes.co.uk

# The customer's always right

I started my first job in 1956 when I was 15 working in a high-class family drapers. I began working in the haberdashery department and worked my way up to the lingerie department. My manageress was a trained corsetiere, which I eventually trained to be too. There was a lot to learn about opera top vests and the voluminous Directoire knickers.

I was also allowed, with a fair amount of verbal coaching, to dress the lingerie window. In those days ours was an island window, which meant you could walk all around it. We would string up bras and girdles all at different heights and drape items over metal stands.

The store was in a town where the Royal Marines had barracks. One day I slipped a dressing gown

June and colleagues dressed as St Trinian's schoolgirls.

off a female mannequin and before I could cover it with a 'modesty sheet', marines were whistling and cheering – mostly at my embarrassment. On another occasion my intimidating superior put me under so much stress that I raced around the window to look at my display not noticing what I'd trodden in on the way. The new pale pink carpet was soiled and smelly – making me very unpopular.

It was a seaside town and it was tradition for businesses to enter a colourful float in the annual carnival. In this photograph we are dressed as St Trinian's schoolgirls, although look how modest we are – no thighs on show!

I still remember the training I received and whenever I help out at charity stalls I treat customers with the same good manners.

**June Male, Cambridgeshire**

## Plant profile

### Arum italicum 'Pictum'

**Height: 30cm**
**Spread: 30cm**
**Conditions: Enjoys moist, heavy soils
and a shady position.**

A great plant with several seasons of interest, it produces attractive green leaves that are heavily marked with cream during the spring, pale green bracts in summer and red berries. It grows well in the moist shady conditions found beneath trees and has an Award of Garden Merit from the RHS. It's available online from specialist growers such as www.dejager.co.uk

## Health tip

### Energy boost

Keep drinking water – at least two litres a day – even though it's turning colder. Your body still needs liquid even if you're not thirsty. If you're just slightly dehydrated you have less energy.

## Senior moment

I received a letter from my solicitor, asking that I call him urgently. I dutifully rang straight away and launched straight in with the information he had asked for. When he eventually managed to butt in he said: "I'm in Egypt at the moment, can I call you when I'm back from my holiday?"

**Marcia Rogers, Mid Glamorgan**

## Fast fact

British actor Albert Finney turned down the role of T E Lawrence in the 1962 film Lawrence of Arabia. The role was given instead to Peter O'Toole who was catapulted into the limelight following the film's huge success. Both actors were in the same class at the Royal Academy of Dramatic Art.

## Small talk

Mark, my four-year-old son, was playing on the lawn with his granddad. Granddad bent over to pick him up exposing his bald patch. "Oh, granddad," cried Mark, "your head's wearing out."

**Mr Carson, Surrey**

## Fashion we wore

I thought readers might be interested in this photograph. I was 19 years old and had just got engaged. We had gone to Blackpool for the day for a treat. I had bought a couple of yards of tartan and made a 'jerkin' – which I'm wearing. I wore it with a black 'Waspie' belt, a white blouse and simple skirt. With the left over tartan I updated my swing-backed 'jigger' coat with an inverted pleat at the back. I covered the three large buttons with the plaid then finished off with floppy tartan bows at the neck.

**Muriel Mcdonagh, Manchester**

# Recipe of the week

## Chocolate cherry trifle
### Serves 4

- ◆ 100 g (4 oz) good quality dark chocolate
- ◆ 400 ml (16 fl oz) Gold Top milk
- ◆ 3 medium egg yolks
- ◆ 2 tbsp caster sugar
- ◆ 4 level tsp cornflour
- ◆ 2-3 drops of vanilla extract
- ◆ 150 g (6 oz) marble cake or chocolate muffins
- ◆ 4-6 tbsp kirsch or cherry brandy
- ◆ 8 tbsp cherry or red fruits compote
- ◆ 284 ml (7 fl oz) pot double cream
- ◆ A handful of fresh cherries, for decoration

1. Grate $1/3$ of the chocolate and set aside for decoration.
2. In a saucepan, heat the milk and rest of chocolate gently until nearly boiling, stirring occasionally.
3. In a large mixing bowl, whisk the egg yolks, sugar, cornflour and vanilla extract. Pour the warm milk into the egg mixture, stir well and pour it back into the pan. Cook over a low heat, stirring to make a smooth, thick custard.
4. Pour the custard into a clean bowl, cover loosely with clingfilm and leave to cool.
5. To assemble the trifle, break up the chocolate cake into chunks and place in a trifle dish. Sprinkle the kirsch or brandy over then spoon in the compote. Spread the cooled custard on top.
6. Whip the cream, adding a little more sugar and alcohol if desired, until it forms soft peaks. Dollop over the custard and chill. Decorate with the grated chocolate and fresh cherries, just before serving.

Recipe: Gold Top milk, www.gold-top.co.uk

# Living my dream

I remember as a boy of six going to see the film Mutiny on the Bounty. I'd always loved those South Sea pictures of waving palm trees and golden sands, so different to the bleak Yorkshire skies. My dear parents worked hard and as I grew up I always thought there must be somewhere over the rainbow, where life could be more fulfilling.

After seeing the film I made up my young mind that the South Seas in the Pacific would be the place for me. My dad, of course, was surprised when I told him that one day I was going to marry a girl with Bounty descendents and live on an island in the Pacific! My chance came when I was offered a job as a set designer in Australia, so I began my adventure.

The picturesque Norfolk Island in the South Pacific.

Here I met my wife Evelyn, who was in fact a descendent of Fletcher Christian of the Bounty. We went on to have two beautiful girls. We lived on an island in the South Sea called Norfolk Island, where the climate was perfect and the scenery stunning. I moved back to England after my wife passed away. I'm now 79 years old and I treasure those wonderful days when my dreams came true.

**John Brook, Weston-Super-Mare**

## Plant profile

### Nerines

**Height: 50cm**
**Spread: 35cm**
**Conditions: Thrive in well-drained soil and a sunny position – they enjoy being baked by the sun.**
Nerines look great against a rustic brick wall, and will enjoy the dry soil at its base. They produce spectacular flowers of red, pink or white – real explosions of colour that brighten the autumn garden. If your soil is heavy, plant them in containers of gritty compost. They're available online from specialist growers such as www.dejager.co.uk, www.jerseyplantsdirect.com and www.vanmeuwen.com

## Health tip
### Take up Tai Chi

If you want to stay healthy this winter try Tai Chi – scientists discovered that it could help boost your immune system. They're not sure why but it could have something to do with Tai Chi's calming nature. Check your local leisure centre for classes in your area.

## Senior moment

I was finding it hard to find a powder puff for a make-up compact until I spotted a set in a chemist. My delight turned to embarrassment when passing them to the cashier I realised my 'puffs' where in fact nipple shields!

**Mrs D Bookfield, S Yorks**

# Fast fact

There are lots of conflicting stories about whether or not The Great Wall of China is visible from space with the naked eye. In 2003 China's own astronaut Yang Liwei said he couldn't see the 5500 mile long structure.

# Small talk

My three-year-old granddaughter was on the beach in St Ives, when she burst into tears. When I asked what was wrong she said: "Those poor little fish in the sea have no toys to play with."

**Hugh Joseph, Cornwall**

# Fashion we wore

**H**ere's a snap of me, my cousin Joyce and my little dog Tony. I'm on the right, aged 18 and Joyce was 16 – it was 1948. Joyce's mum made the dresses, which we thought made us look so lovely. They were made of cotton and had quite a nice, new style to them. Joyce and I were evacuated from Manchester to Staffordshire, for four years, which we enjoyed – apart from missing our parents of course.

**Lilian Morrissey, Stockport**

# Recipe of the week

## Chantenay vegetable chilli

**Serves 4**

- ◆ 1 tbsp olive oil
- ◆ 1 onion, chopped
- ◆ 2 cloves garlic, crushed
- ◆ 250 g (10 oz) Chantenay carrots, whole and unpeeled
- ◆ 350 g (14 oz) frozen mixed vegetables
- ◆ 2 tsp ground cumin
- ◆ 2 tsp ground coriander
- ◆ 2 tsp dried oregano
- ◆ 1-2 tsp dried chilli flakes
- ◆ 1 tsp paprika
- ◆ 400 g (16 oz) can of mixed beans
- ◆ 400 g (16 oz) can of chopped tomatoes
- ◆ 300 ml (12 fl oz) boiling water
- ◆ Salt and pepper

To serve:
- ◆ 100 ml (4 fl oz) sour cream or crème fraîche
- ◆ A handful of fresh coriander leaves, roughly chopped

1. In a large saucepan, gently fry the onion in the oil for 5 minutes, or until soft. Add the garlic and fry for a further minute.
2. Next, add the carrots, mixed vegetables and the spices and fry for a further 2-3 minutes, or until spicy aromas rise from the pan.
3. Finally add the beans, tinned tomatoes and boiling water and bring up to the boil. Cover and simmer for 20-25 minutes, or until the vegetables are tender. Check after 15 minutes and if the sauce seems a little thin uncover for the remaining cooking time.
4. Serve immediately sprinkled with the coriander and a dollop of sour cream or crème fraîche. Goes well with boiled rice or as a jacket potato topping.

Recipe: Chantenay Carrots, www.chantenay.co.uk/

# I remember Two-Way Family Favourites

## BY: MARION CLARKE

For all of us who grew up in the Fifties, Sunday dinner will always be linked in our minds with listening to Two-Way Family Favourites. The distinctive aroma of roast beef and well-boiled cabbage went hand-in-hand with the familiar announcement: "The time in Britain is twelve noon, in Germany it's one o'clock, but home and away it's time for Two-Way Family Favourites" followed by the signature tune With a Song in My Heart played by Andre Kostelanetz and his orchestra.

The programme had its origin in the Second World War when it was known as Forces Favourites and went out on Tuesday evenings. Families could request a record along with a dedication for relatives who were serving with the British Forces overseas. After the war it was moved to Sundays and expanded from 30 to 90 minutes. In keeping with its Sunday slot, Auntie Beeb raised the moral tone by forbidding noisy jazz, unseemly banter, and any mention of girlfriends or fiancées.

## It was known as Forces Favourites...

Despite these constraints, Two-Way Family Favourites proved to be hugely popular, attracting an audience of 16 million listeners at its peak. National Service meant that most people had a friend or relative in the army, navy or air force but its popularity was also due to the fact that it was one of the few daytime programmes playing the original versions of popular records. (In the evenings, pop fans could tune in to Radio Luxembourg.)

Anne Shelton, Dickie Valentine and Ruby Murray – all big stars of the era – were regularly heard on the show along with much-loved novelty numbers such as The Railroad Runs Through the Middle of the House, Where Will the Baby's Dimple Be? and How Much is That Doggie in the Window? Rarely a week passed without a soulful rendition of O Mein Papa being played at the request of a homesick son or daughter.

The formula was to have one presenter based in London and the other in a BFPO (British Forces Posted Overseas) station which might be West Germany,

Stars like Ruby Murray were eagerly listened to.

Singapore, Hong Kong, Canada or Australia. Over the years, Two-Way Family Favourites had many well-known presenters including Judith Chalmers, Michael Aspel, Bill Crozier and Sarah Kennedy, but the two best-remembered ones are Jean Metcalfe and Cliff Michelmore who fell in love over the air waves and were married in March 1950. Naturally, no hint of romance was allowed to appear on the programme but the secret was eventually leaked and a listener left Jean £3,000 which the couple used to buy a home in Reigate.

Eventually, Two-Way Family Favourites was moved from the BBC Light Programme to Radio 2 until it was finally axed in 1970.

# Quiz of the month

All these events took place in the month of October over the past 60 years, but can you arrange them in the order that they happened?

PIC REX FEATURES

**A** Two people have been killed and at least 75 injured in rioting sparked by the admission of James Meredith, a black American, to the University of Mississippi.

**B** There has been a direct bomb attack on the British Government at the Conservative party conference in Brighton.

**C** The seven-sided 50p coin comes into circulation to replace the 10-shilling note.

**D** The oil company British Petroleum announces it has struck oil in the North Sea.

**E** The Mary Rose, flagship of King Henry VIII, has been raised to the surface after 437 years at the bottom of the Solent.

**F** The Campaign for Nuclear Disarmament (CND) has held its biggest ever protest against nuclear missiles in London with an estimated one million people taking part.

**G** Princess Margaret has called off her wedding to Group Captain Peter Townsend.

**H** More than 130 people, mainly children, are killed when a coal slag heap collapses at Aberfan in Wales.

**I** Jeffrey Archer has resigned as Deputy Chairman of the Conservative Party following allegations that he tried to pay a prostitute to go abroad to avoid a scandal.

**J** The Guildford Four have been released. Their convictions were quashed by the Court of Appeal after 15 years in prison.

**K** Former Liberal leader, Jeremy Thorpe, has denied any involvement in a plot to kill one time friend Norman Scott and suggestions that he had a homosexual relationship with the former male model.

**L** Former champion jockey, Lester Piggott, has been sentenced to three years imprisonment after being found guilty of a £3m tax fraud.

**M** Cardinals at the Vatican have chosen the first non-Italian Pope for more than 400 years. Catholics around the world have been astonished by the choice of Cardinal Karol Wojtyla, the Archbishop of Krakow.

**N** British Rail began its new high speed train service. The Inter-City 125 arrived three minutes early on its first journey from London to Bristol.

**O** Britain's first independent radio station, LBC (London Broadcasting Company), began broadcasting on VHF and medium wave.

**P** Actors Richard Burton and Elizabeth Taylor have secretly remarried in Africa only 16 months after getting divorced.

News stories taken from http://news.bbc.co.uk/onthisday/

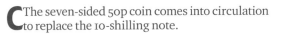

ANSWERS: G) 1955, A) 1962, H) 1966, C) 1969, D) 1970, O) 1973, P) 1975, N) 1976, K) 1977, M) 1977, E) 1978, F) 1982, B) 1983, I) 1984, L) 1986, J) 1989

# Here comes the bride?

BY: TONY BRIDGLAND

## The groom and best man are on time – but where are the guests?

**B**rian put his tousled head round my bedroom door. "You'd better get up, mate," he said. "Time's getting on."

I yawned and stretched, drew back the curtains and peered out. It was raining. It didn't look like a good day for my wedding.

A careful shave – I didn't want unsightly nicks on my chin. I put a Windsor knot in my blue Co-op tie, then had a slice of toast. I didn't feel like eating much. I asked Brian for the umpteenth time if he had got the ring in his pocket.

Hunched against the drizzle, we made our way to the bus stop. Seated on the top deck, we lit cigarettes and stared out of the blurred windows.

The church clock said twenty to as we hurried up the path. There was nobody inside. We took off our wet macs and draped them over a pew.

"What's the time?" I asked Brian, needlessly. He shot the cuffs of his new rayon shirt and looked at his new watch (£2 out of the catalogue). "Just turned twenty to. People should be arriving soon."

Minutes ticked by. Nobody came. We stood in the porch and had another fag. The rain had plastered our hair flat to our heads and our carnations had been crushed by our macs.

"You sure it's today?" asked Brian.

"Course I am," I said.

## "Not very good light for the photographs"

"Not very good light today for the photographs, is it?" Brian looked at his watch again. He had always had a knack of adding more gloom to an already fraught situation.

"Where the hell is everybody?" I almost screamed.

"Ssshhh," Brian remonstrated. "You're in church."

All kinds of thoughts raced through my mind. Had Jennifer been in an accident? Even if she had, where were all the other people? Uncle Ted and Aunt Sylvia would be driving down from Luton in their new Ford Popular, bought with a modest £400 win on Vernons Pools.

What if Jennifer had changed her mind? We'd had a tiff about the date of the wedding. Jennifer had wanted it in June but we had left it too late. Jennifer said she didn't mind if we postponed it until the following year, but I pointed out that I could be called up for National Service at any time. She burst into tears and agreed to make it the earliest available Saturday, which turned out to be October.

Surely Jennifer wouldn't back out without telling me? No – it was more likely her mother. She never had liked me, her mother. Ever since the first time I went to Sunday tea and Jennifer's father had said he thought the ham tasted a bit off and, tactlessly, I had agreed with him.

**S**he had never thought I was good enough for her daughter, with my lowly aspirations of becoming a plumber. Not like her son Roger, who was training to be an accountant and played badminton. My idea of sporting activity was a game of darts with Brian down at The Two Sawyers.

"It's turned quarter past," announced Brian. He had been pacing up and down the big stone slabs, muttering, 'I just don't bloody understand this at all', forgetting his reproach to me about swearing in church. He footsteps echoed in the emptiness.

He said: "Come on, mate, let's go outside and have another fag."

"What do you want to do then?" he asked as we stood in the porch, staring at the downpour.

"Give it another ten minutes," I answered, fighting back the tears and sucking on my damp Woodbine. "Then if nobody comes we'll go down the Sawyer's and have a pint."

Grinding our dog-ends into the ancient granite steps, we trooped back inside and sat silently in the front pew.

Suddenly there was a clatter of hurrying feet. But it wasn't a wedding guest. A middle-aged man in a cassock, red-faced from running, rushed past us and up the stairs to the organ loft. We heard banging and a few minutes later he reappeared and spotted us.

"Phew!" he puffed. "Just in time."

"What do you mean, just in time?" we asked.

"It's the wife," he explained. "Been up all night

PIC: KATE DAVIES

# The feeling of relief was indescribable.

with one of her blinking migraines. I clean forgot I'd got to put the ruddy clocks back. And there's a wedding in 25 minutes. Is that why you're here?"

I looked at Brian. He looked at me. The feeling of relief was indescribable. "You great steaming twerp!" I shouted. "You forgot to put that blooming catalogue thing of yours back as well."

He gave a pallid grin and put his arm round my shoulder whereupon we both burst into hysterical laughter.

With poetic timing, the rain stopped and a feeble autumnal sun was shining. A group of people were coming in through the church gates. Uncle Ted and Aunt Sylvia were parking their gleaming Ford Popular across the street.

Jennifer arrived on her father's arm, looking beautiful. We had a lovely wedding. Everybody laughed at Brian's speech, which was mostly about our day so far. Jennifer's dad shook my hand and gave me a £50 cheque. Even her mother treated me to a thin-lipped kiss.

The photographs came out fine. One still adorns our sideboard. If you look carefully you can see that my carnation has nearly all of its petals missing. We often laugh about that.

# November 2010

Monday

1

All Saints' Day

Tuesday

2

Wednesday

3

Thursday

4

Friday

5

Guy Fawkes' Night

Saturday

6

Sunday

7

Monday

8

Tuesday

9

Wednesday

10

Thursday

11

Friday

12

Saturday

13

Sunday

14

Remembrance Sunday

Monday

15

Tuesday

16

Wednesday

17

Thursday

18

Friday

19

Saturday

20

Sunday

21

Monday

22

| Tuesday | Saturday |
|---|---|
| **23** | **27** |
| Wednesday | Sunday |
| **24** | **28** |
| Thursday | Monday |
| **25** | **29** |
| Friday | Tuesday |
| **26** | **30** |
| | St Andrew's Day (Bank Holiday Scotland) |

## Poetry corner

# Nature's rest

The season's changed, Autumn has gone,
Along with it many a bird's song.
Plant and tree closing down their heads,
Putting their growing away to bed.

The leaves have fallen, except the beech,
Its pruning time for those we can reach.
The mower's been oiled and put away,
Having a rest until another spring day.

The grass has stopped growing upon the lawn,
The trees are looking bare and forlorn.
Beautiful fruit picked and put in store,
To see us through the winter, we'll not want more.

The Christmas tree, four years ago,
Too big for indoors, was left out to grow.
Now, it's wide and eight foot ten,
Never to be brought indoors again.

**Gerald Cosens, Amotherby**

PIC: REX FEATURES

## My sister

**M**y sister Pam and I were evacuated together at the beginning of the war. We went to live with a married couple on a farm in Newton Stacey. Also billeted with us were two Land Girls. Being 'townies' we were fascinated by their uniforms and their work on the farm.

After the war in 1947 and as soon she was old enough, Pam joined the Women's Land Army where she stayed for three years. She was taught to drive a three tonne lorry and was made a forewoman. She has recently received her Land Army badge and certificate along with an invitation to attend a reunion of the Hampshire branch of the Women's Land Army.

Left: Pam in her uniform in 1947
Right: Pam, now 80, with Daisy her Land Army doll.

Last year Pam celebrated her 80th birthday and I gave her a doll called Daisy dressed in Land Army uniform, which I knitted from a pattern printed in Yours some years ago.

**Dorothy Davies, Portsmouth**

## Plant profile

### Rudbeckia fulgida 'Goldsturm'

**Height: 60cm**
**Spread: 50cm**
**Conditions: Thrives in sunny well-drained soils.**
The large, daisy–like flowers of 'Goldsturm' are great in a late summer border, complementing perfectly the autumnal shades of the trees – with bright yellow petals that really set the garden ablaze. It starts flowering in August and may still be blooming in November. Short enough not to require staking, it's popular with many gardeners and has an Award of Garden Merit from the RHS. Widely available from garden centres.

## Health tip
### Bookworm

Spare half an hour to curl up with your favourite book, your brain will thank you. Studies show that bookworms out perform people with lower reading levels on cognitive tests.

## Senior moment

A friend's 84-year-old uncle made an appointment with his doctor and duly turned up at the correct time and date. "Good morning, Mr Thompson," said the GP. "What can I do for you today?" He looked a bit perplexed and admitted to the doctor that he couldn't remember. "That's all right," said the GP. "I'll just take your blood pressure while you think about it!"　**Mrs H Gillen, by email**

## Fast fact

50 per cent of the heat in our homes is lost through the roof and walls. According to the Energy Saving Trust poorly insulated roofs and walls are the culprits of enough wasted energy to heat nearly 1.9 million homes for a year.

## Small talk

Recently we took our three-year-old grandson out in the car. When I bemoaned the fact that we had forgotten the buggy, he piped up and said: "I have got two legs you know!"

**P Wood, Wirral**

## Fashion we wore

This picture, taken in 1958, is of me in my first grown-up outfit. The full skirt was made in lilac-coloured cotton with figures of teddy boys and girls, edged in black, around the bottom. I bought it from my mum's mail order catalogue and it cost me £2 14s 6d. As I was only earning £2 11s 9d, working 48 hours a week in a shop, it took me ages to pay off the debt. But I didn't mind – with a net petticoat underneath the skirt and a pair of cute kitten heels I felt like I was the height of fashion.

**Gillian Wood, Salisbury**

## Recipe of the week

### Easy Lincolnshire carrot pudding
**Serves 6-8**

- ◆ 100 g (4 oz) plain flour
- ◆ ½ tsp bicarbonate of soda
- ◆ 1 tsp mixed spice
- ◆ 100 g (4 oz) suet
- ◆ 100 g (4 oz) raisins
- ◆ 100 g (4 oz) currants
- ◆ 100 g (4 oz) potato, grated
- ◆ 100 g (4 oz) carrots, grated
- ◆ 100 g (4 oz) demerara sugar
- ◆ 100 g (4 oz) fine breadcrumbs
- ◆ 25 g (1 oz) chopped glacé cherries
- ◆ 1 large egg, beaten

1. Lightly grease a large pudding basin. In a mixing bowl, combine the flour, bicarbonate of soda and mixed spice. Add all the other ingredients except the egg, and stir thoroughly until fully combined.
2. Add the egg and bind well. If the mixture is a little too stiff, add a tablespoon of milk. Pour into the basin, leaving some space at the top, as it will expand during cooking.
3. Cover the top with a double layer of grease proof paper and tie with string to secure. Steam for 3 hours.
4. Leave to stand for 5 minutes and serve with lashings of custard, brandy sauce or double cream.

Recipe: British Carrots, www.britishcarrots.co.uk

# Autograph hunting

It all started when I was a young girl on a trip to London visiting my father's aunt and uncle and their daughter, Peggy, who worked for the BBC. She suggested we went to the studios in Lime Grove to see if we could get any autographs. From that day my cousin Tessa and I would often be found outside the stage door of The Winter Garden Theatre in Bournemouth waiting for autographs.

Over the years I was lucky enough to get dated autographs from George Formby, Bernard Miles and The Beverley Sisters – who we loved. And also from many famous comedians including Bob Monkhouse and Bruce Forsyth as well as many singers including Andy Williams, Johnny Mathis, Tony Bennett, Johnny Cash and June Carter. Not forgetting the lovely Perry Como who was a perfect gentleman.

Cliff Richard backstage at the London Palladium.

Alma Cogan and Petula Cark were also lovely.

More recently I've got autographs from Shirley Bassey, Diana Ross, Lulu and Cilla Black. There was a large queue waiting for Cilla and, as I was expecting at the time, her husband Bobby found me a chair to sit on – what a lovely man.

I've always loved Cliff Richard and in 1974 I had the opportunity to meet him backstage at the London Palladium. While there the telephone rang and he picked it up saying "Hello, London Palladium stage door." I often wonder who was on the other end, what a surprise that must have been.

**Jackie Wright, Poole**

## Plant profile

### Hibiscus 'Fireglow'

**Height: 30cm**

**Spread: 30cm**

**Conditions: Thrives on a sunny windowsill – one of the few flowering houseplants that cope with a south-facing position.**

Tender varieties of hibiscus are popular houseplants as they flower repeatedly throughout the year. The 10cm coral-red blooms of this variety will add a splash of colour. If the plant becomes leggy, prune it hard and feed it well. Ensure the compost remains moist during the growing season but that it almost dries out between waterings at other times.

## Health tip
### Have a cuppa

Drinking three or four cups or two mugs of tea a day could help you to fight off heart disease and boost your brain power. The benefits are all down to the antioxidant polyphenols that are found in tealeaves. The even better news is that adding milk doesn't hamper the effects.

## Senior moment

I wear contact lenses and one morning, when putting them in, I couldn't find the one for my left eye. After searching high and low, I realised that I had put both lenses in my right eye – one on top of the other!

**Jeanette Miles, Kent**

## Fast fact

Daily broadcasting from the BBC began on November 14, 1922, from a studio in London. The British Broadcasting Company was originally formed by a group of leading wireless manufacturers, including the great pioneer Marconi, with the aim of promoting the sale of radio sets.

## Small talk

I had to laugh when a friend's little boy was handed a cowboy outfit for his birthday. "Gosh, thanks a million," he said, "is the horse outside?"
**Mrs Evans, Denbighshire**

## Fashion we wore

Here are a couple of my favourite photos. The bride in the picture is, of course, me! It was taken September 21, 1940, the day before my 21st birthday – I'm not sure where the bridegroom was at the time! The other photo is earlier – 1937 or 38. I imagine I'm dressed for a dance because we used to go to all the big dances in Bath as we lived near the centre of the city. My husband wasn't fit enough to go into the forces in the war, but he worked hard in the police and wholesale food business. When he went out on patrol during the bombing we were never sure if we were going to see each other again but we were the lucky ones.
**Lilian Strong, Trowbridge**

## Recipe of the week

### Quick mid-week roast
**Serves 4**

- ◆ 1 tbsp olive oil
- ◆ 8 chicken thighs, skin on
- ◆ 300 g (12 oz) carrots, cut into 3 cm (1¼ in) pieces
- ◆ 2 large parsnips, cut into 3 cm (1¼ in) wedges
- ◆ 750 g (1 lb 8 oz) King Edward potatoes, cut into wedges
- ◆ 1 tbsp thyme leaves
- ◆ 1 tbsp honey
- ◆ 2 tbsp Worcestershire sauce

1. Preheat the oven to 200C/400°F/Gas Mark 6. In a large frying pan, heat the oil and fry the chicken for 2 minutes on each side. Transfer to a large roasting tin with all the vegetables.
2. Stir in the thyme, honey and Worcestershire sauce.
3. Bake for 30 minutes and then remove from the oven to drain off and reserve most of the excess juice. Return to the oven for a further 10 minutes.
4. Meanwhile, make gravy with the reserved juices. Serve immediately while still piping hot.

Recipe: Love Potatoes, www.britishpotatoes.co.uk

# Our Guide troop

Elizabeth (second from left on bottom row) with the 16th Kuala Lumpur Girl Guide troop.

**W**e arrived in Kuala Lumpur, Malaya in 1955, moving into an army base, which was surrounded by a double perimeter fence and had armed sentries at the gate. At the time Malaya was fighting a guerrilla war and the armed forces were heavily involved with our school.

School started at eight in the morning and finished just after noon and lots of our lessons were held outside. We travelled to school in a large caged army truck. Our school later became Bourne School, after Sir Geoffrey Bourne.

Wednesday was Girl Guides day and our troop was called the 16th Kuala Lumpur. It was made up of the daughters of army and airforce men and was the only British troupe in Malaya. Our head girl was called Toni Gardiner, who went on to marry King Hussein of Jordan.

We had a great time at Guides doing the usual activities, but all with a slight difference. When making fire we'd have to be careful that we were picking up small sticks and not small snakes. Our motto became, 'If your stick moves drop it!' We'd go into the jungle for trail-finding and doing woodcraft, but we made so much noise that anything with four legs got out of the way and we ignored the hissing sounds which came down from the trees. Although we had more freedom back them, we were aware we were guests in another country, so we were always well-behaved in our uniforms.

**Elizabeth Johnston, Dumfries**

## Plant profile

### Sempervivums

**Height: 10cm**
**Spread: 15cm**
**Conditions: Thrives in extremely well-drained soil and a sunny position.**

Few plants thrive on neglect, but house–leeks, as sempervivums are commonly called, do. Plant them in a shallow terracotta bowl using a mixture of gravel, grit and compost and they'll look colourful all year round – even more so during the summer when conical spikes of greenish pink flowers emerge. Alternatively, place them in paving cracks or in a strawberry planter. Several varieties have a RHS Award of Garden Merit.

## Health tip
### Brush up

Look after your teeth and gums or you could harm your heart. Experts warn that bleeding gums allow bacteria from your mouth to enter your bloodstream. It sticks to your blood platelets and could lead to blood clots and a heart attack or stroke. So care for your teeth and see your dentist regularly.

## Senior moment

I carefully poached pears in white wine, then put them in a dish and poured over a mushroom sauce. Not a recipe I can recommend but a bowl of mushroom sauce and bowl of custard did look alike in the fridge!

**J Thompson, Kent**

## Fast fact

Cattle (particularly bulls) are, in fact, red-green colour blind despite the commonly held belief that bulls are enraged and charge towards the colour red. The myth stems from bullfighting when the matador waves a red cape. It's actually the movement of the fabric that irritates them not the red colour.

## Small talk

A friend was selling his car and I asked him how much he wanted for it. "About two thousand nicker," he replied. My granddaughter Katie asked: "Why does he want two thousand knickers for it? What's he going to do with them all?"

**Melanie Lee, Kent**

## Fashion we wore

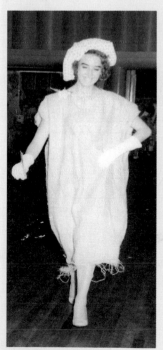

In this photo I'm wearing a 'sack' dress (which was actually made out of a sack)! It was 1957 – I was 19 at the time and on holiday in Jersey. I entered one of the competitions on the holiday camp – it was to wear something 'in vogue'. I can't remember if I won and I'm not sure what people would think of the outfit these days. I'm not too sure about those high heels either – I only wear them these days if I don't have to walk very far.

**Doreen Leonard, Mill Hill, London**

## Recipe of the week

### The ultimate fudge
Makes 30-40 pieces

- 397 g (16 fl oz) can Carnation condensed milk
- 150 ml (¼ pt) milk
- 450 g (1 lb) demerara sugar
- 125 g (5 oz) butter

Optional ingredients:
- 150 g (6o z) glacé cherries, halved and 50 g (2 oz) stem ginger, chopped
- 150 g (6 oz) dark chocolate, chopped and 75 g (3 oz) hazelnuts, toasted
- 150 g (6 oz) raisins soaked in 3 tbsp rum

1. Grease and base line a 20 cm (8 inch) square tin with baking parchment.
2. In a large non-stick saucepan, gently heat the basic ingredients stirring continuously until the sugar dissolves completely.
3. Bring to the boil and simmer for 10-15 minutes, stirring and scraping the base of the pan continuously.
4. Test if the fudge is ready by dropping a little of the mixture into a jug of ice-cold water – if a soft ball of fudge is formed it is ready.
5. Remove immediately from the heat and beat the fudge for about 10 minutes, or until it is thick and grainy.
6. Gently stir in the optional ingredients, if using. Pour into the prepared tin and leave to cool before cutting into squares.

Recipe: Nestlé Carnation, www.carnation.co.uk

# Wartime memories

**D**uring the war we lived in the country, about six miles from Derby. Dad was in the Air Raid Precautions (ARP) and as soon as he heard the sirens he'd be off on his bicycle to Derby for his duties. Mother was left at home with us four children.

We had an air-raid shelter in our garden, but we only went into it on one occasion – it was too much for mother to get four sleepy children down there on her own. Dad had noticed many families had been found safe under staircases, so we had a bunk bed built under our stairs and that was our shelter whenever the siren sounded.

Our grandparents lived in Ilkeston and we'd sometimes shop there, but we always had to be

A wartime garden shelter was the safest option for many families but it could be a difficult night-time trip.

back before dark. At dark the searchlights would start up in the sky, which was quite scary as the Rolls Royce factory in Derby was always being sought out by the bombers.

I remember picking up strips of silver-like foil, in the fields around us. These had been dropped by our aircrafts to confuse the enemy planes. Then there were the barrage balloons – they looked huge to us small children. Dad always told us if we were out on our bikes down the lane and an aircraft flew over we were to get into the roadside ditch as it could be one of the enemies.

**Sally Roberts, Cheshire**

## Plant profile

### Sclumbergera x buckleyi

**Height: 30cm**
**Spread: 30cm**
**Conditions: These cacti thrive in direct sunlight or partial shade and well-drained, gritty compost.**
Christmas cacti produce vibrant red, cerise or white flowers at the end of arching stems right through the winter months. They're a great choice for brightening an empty windowsill and the stems look charming trailing over the sides of a wicker hanging basket. Water regularly and feed weekly during the growing season. Widely available from garden centres.

## Health tip
### Beat festive stress

A massive 40 per cent of us feel increasingly anxious and stressed as Christmas approaches. Try to plan ahead now and, if you're feeling overwhelmed, make time to talk to someone and ask for help with all your festive plans. If it all gets too much call Mind on 0845 766 0163.

## Senior moment

I went into the Post Office and asked for a second-hand stamp book. The clerk looked blank, then hunted for a strip of stamps. "Will these do?" he said. "They've been stamped twice."

**Ivy Musk, Essex**

PIC GETTY IMAGES

## Fast fact

The Queen and the Duke of Edinburgh were married in Westminster Abbey on November 20, 1947 in front of 2000 invited guests. The two kneelers, used during the service, were made from orange boxes, due to post-wartime austerity and covered in rose pink silk. Their wedding cake had four tiers and was nine feet high.

## Small talk

My daughter was talking to a very pregnant friend when she turned to my grandson, who is three years old, and said: "Look Dylan, my friend has a baby in her tummy." After some thought my grandson said: "Did she eat her baby?"

**Mrs R Bedford, Gloucestershire**

## Fashion we wore

Here's a picture of me and my husband, Patrick, taken on the 'Lovers Seat' in Hastings. It was 1951 – the year we got engaged. The dress I'm wearing is brown and white cotton – I remember that I loved that dress because it always looked very smart and I felt a million dollars in it. I'm also wearing white cotton gloves and brown wedge shoes (which you can't see in the photo).

**Daphne Collins, Croydon**

## Recipe of the week

### Creamy potato and mushroom gratin
Serves 4

- ◆ 25 g (1 oz) butter
- ◆ 1 tbsp olive oil
- ◆ 350 g (14 oz) assorted mushroom, sliced
- ◆ 1 clove garlic, crushed
- ◆ ¹/₂ tsp freshly grated nutmeg
- ◆ 675 g (1 lb 7 oz) potatoes, peeled
- ◆ 450 g (1 lb) sweet potatoes, peeled
- ◆ 300 ml (¹/₂ pt) full fat milk
- ◆ 50 g (2 oz) Cheddar cheese, grated
- ◆ Salt and pepper

1. Preheat the oven to 180°C/350°F/Gas Mark 4. In a large frying pan, heat the butter and oil together before adding the mushrooms. Cook over a high heat until the mushrooms have softened and the juices evaporated. Stir in the garlic and nutmeg and remove from the heat.

2. Slice the potatoes to the thickness of a pound coin. Arrange half over the base of a lightly greased 1.4 litre (2½ pt) ovenproof dish and season well. Scatter over half of the mushrooms and repeat the layers.

3. Pour the milk over, cover the dish with foil and bake for 1 hour.

4. Remove from the oven, scatter over the cheese and bake for a further 15 minutes, or until the top is golden brown and the potatoes are fully cooked.

5. Serve with crusty bread for a warming supper or as an accompaniment to a Sunday roast.

◆ **Top tip:** 'Economy' mushrooms taste just as good in this dish and helps to cut costs. Add some sliced bacon to the dish to make it a more substantial meal.

Recipe: Mushroom Bureau, www.mushroom-uk.com

# I dreamed of millions

I always dreamed of being a millionaire with a large house in the country. I'd have travelled the world, had fabulous parties, owned pedigree dogs and settled down with three children.

The reality was coming from Hull and a working class background, I took the first office job I could and my life followed a very different path. I was low paid, but content. I managed to follow part of my dream and travel a lot, albeit package-type tours, but still I travelled. I made the most of my single years, partied and then in time I settled down and had my three children. Over the years our family has enjoyed the company of various pets including hamsters, gerbils, rabbits and dogs. I gave up office work not long after my son was born and began child-minding instead, which was so much more rewarding.

A very contented Janette with her Westies.

Now that I'm 50 I feel as though I've fulfilled all of my dreams. I have three wonderful children and a lovely house in a small country village. A few years back I fulfilled another part of my dream when I bought two beautiful West Highland White terriers.

I'm happy with what I've achieved. People change as do their dreams, but although I'm not a millionaire I am content. After all, there is more than one way to be rich.

**Janette Hancock, East Riding of Yorkshire**

## Plant profile

### African violet

**Height: 15cm**

**Spread: 15cm**

**Conditions: Thrives if planted in a container of well-drained compost and placed on a bright windowsill.**

Few houseplants are as popular as the African violet, or Saintpaulia. It's a great choice if you're a novice gardener as it copes well with neglect and will flower on and off throughout the year. It likes cool, dry conditions so a west-facing window is ideal. But never over-water – an African violet is much happier drying out than being waterlogged. Widely available from garden centres.

## Health tip
### Indulge

One item you can really tuck into this Christmas is the cranberry sauce – especially if it's homemade. Cranberries are full of antioxidants and special compounds, which could help to prevent urinary tract infections such as cystitis.

## Senior moment

I had just come out of hospital and my husband offered to do the shopping. I gave him a list, together with a couple of cards to post. When he came back the shopping had doubled. He confessed that he had to try to remember what was on the list because he'd posted it along with the cards!

**Pam West, Dorset**

## Fast fact

We blink up to 15 times a minute and each blink lasts between 100 and 150 milliseconds. We automatically blink when we hear a loud sudden noise, to protect our eyes. The cornea, the transparent covering at the front of the eye, is the only living tissue in the human body that doesn't contain any blood vessels.

## Small talk

I was visiting my daughter recently and we were all going out for a meal. My granddaughter was watching intently as I applied my make up and then sprayed my hair. "Why did you do that grandma?" she asked. "To keep my hair in place," I replied. She couldn't resist touching it: "Oh grandma that feels like shredded wheat."

**Mary Green, Cumbria**

## Fashion we wore

I thought you might like to see this picture of my wedding in 1956 (to my first husband, now sadly deceased). The dress was made for me by a friend out of ten yards of figured taffeta, which cost me 10s a yard. My veil came from Gibraltar – it was two and a half yards wide and five yards long. After we were married, both the dress and veil were loaned out on many occasions to friends and family – so we got plenty of value out of it. I eventually sold it a few years ago on an internet auction site, so hopefully someone, somewhere is still getting the use out of it.

**Mooneen Truckle, Salisbury**

## Recipe of the week

### Last minute Christmas cake
Serves 10-12

- ◆ 675 g (1 lb 7 oz) mixed dried fruits
- ◆ 75 g (3 oz) glacé cherries, quartered
- ◆ Zest and juice of 1 lemon
- ◆ Zest and juice of 1 orange
- ◆ 4 tbsp dark rum or brandy
- ◆ 225 g (9 oz) butter, softened
- ◆ 225 g (9 oz) light soft brown sugar
- ◆ 4 large Lion Quality eggs, beaten
- ◆ 225 g (9 oz) plain flour
- ◆ $\frac{1}{2}$ tsp mixed ground spice
- ◆ $\frac{1}{2}$ tsp ground cinnamon
- ◆ 50 g (2 oz) flaked almonds

To decorate:
- ◆ 4 tbsp apricot jam, sieved
- ◆ 22 walnut halves
- ◆ 20 blanched almonds

1. Preheat the oven to 170°C/325°F/Gas Mark 3. Line and grease a 20 cm (8 inch) deep round cake tin.
2. In a medium saucepan, mix the first four ingredients and bring to the boil. Remove from the heat and stir in the alcohol. Leave to cool.
3. Use a food processor to purée one third of the fruit.
4. In a large mixing bowl, cream the butter and sugar together with an electric whisk until soft and fluffy. Gradually add the eggs, beating well between each addition. Sift in the flour and spices.
5. Finally, stir in the fruit purée, flaked almonds and rest of fruits. Spoon into the tin and tap to level the surface. Bake for 2-2½ hours, or until a skewer comes out clean. Leave to cool before removing from the tin. Peel away the lining paper and place on a serving plate or cake stand.
6. To decorate, heat the jam in a small pan until runny. Brush over the top of the cake, arrange the nuts, and brush over any remaining jam.

Recipe: British Lion Eggs, www.eggrecipes.co.uk

# I remember Woolworth's

BY: MARION CLARKE

For almost a century, Woolworth's was a familiar sight on every high street in the country. Although the idea for 'five-and-dime' stores originated in America, F W Woolworth rapidly became a British institution after the first shop opened in Liverpool in 1909 – when queues formed to buy everything from glassware to tin toys.

Mass production meant that Woolworth's was able to sell products more cheaply than its competitors, but British customers were wary of the unfamiliar store layout which was designed to encourage shoppers to browse the aisles. To lure them in, the refreshment rooms offered free pots of tea for the first year of trading.

It worked – and the British offshoot became more successful than its American parent. By the 1930s Woolworth stores were opening at the rate of one every

## Woolies appealed to all the family

fortnight, bringing the total up to 759 branches by outbreak of the Second World War. The company was able to keep to its pricing policy of 3d and 6d by breaking down more expensive items into parts so, for example, a teapot would cost 6d and

The bargain store became a British institution until its sad demise.

PIC: GETTY IMAGES

its lid sold for 3d.

Woolies appealed to all the family. Housewives went for bargains like bags of broken biscuits while men headed for its range of cheap tools, screws and cycle parts and children spent their pocket money on Pick 'n' Mix sweets.

The long rows of counters offered all of life's necessities from brown paper and string to rose bushes and garden furniture. It was even celebrated in verse; in Stanley Holloway's well-loved monologue, Albert and the Lion, Albert brandishes a stick with a horse's head handle that is 'the finest that Woolworth's could sell'.

After the war, inflation drove Woolworth prices up

and its 'Nothing over sixpence' (or 'Nix over Six') slogan had to be abandoned but the store continued to thrive. It introduced its own brand of clothing, named Winfield after the middle name of its founder, Frank Winfield Woolworth.

Generations of teenagers bought their first records in Woolworth's even though in the 1960s it didn't sell chart music. Instead, its Embassy record label offered cheap cover versions by unknown artists, so Beatles fans had to settle for A Hard Day's Night sung by The Typhoons.

The wonder of Woolies came to an end when its doors finally closed in January 2009 and people mourned the bargain store that had always been part of their lives.

# Quiz of the month

All these events took place in the month of November over the past 60 years, but can you arrange them in the order that they happened?

PIC: REX FEATURES

**A** An estimated jackpot of £7m may be won in Britain's first ever lottery draw. A £1 ticket gives you a one-in-14-million chance of striking lucky.

**B** Bookshops all over England sell out of the controversial novel Lady Chatterley's Lover

**C** Democrat Bill Clinton has won the election to become the 42nd president of United States and the first in US history born after World War Two.

**D** Detectives are searching for British aristocrat Lord Lucan, following the murder of his children's nanny and an attack on his estranged wife.

**E** Freddie Mercury, the lead singer for rock group Queen, has died aged 45, just one day after he publicly announced he was HIV positive.

**F** Guinness Book of Records co-founder and editor Ross McWhirter has been shot dead outside his North London home.

**G** John F Kennedy, the President of the United States, has been assassinated by a gunman in Dallas, Texas. He was hit in the head and throat when three shots were fired at his open-topped car.

**H** John Major is to be Britain's new Prime Minister after winning the Conservative leadership election.

**I** The Berlin Wall has been breached after nearly three decades keeping East and West Berliners apart.

**J** The Conservative Government has frozen pay and prices in an attempt to halt spiralling inflation.

**K** The English pound note is to disappear after more than 150 years.

**L** The Labour Party has chosen the outspoken left-wing MP, Michael Foot, as its new leader.

**M** The Queen Mother has had her right hip replaced in an operation in London. Her doctors have said she is making a good recovery.

**N** The Rhodesian Government, led by Prime Minister Ian Smith, has illegally severed links with the British Crown.

**O** The Soviet Union has launched the first ever living creature into the cosmos. The dog, described as a female Russian breed, was projected into space aboard Sputnik II.

**P** The wedding of the Queen's only daughter, Princess Anne, has taken place at Westminster Abbey. Princess Anne, 23, married Mark Phillips, a lieutenant in the Army.

News stories taken from http://news.bbc.co.uk/onthisday/

Answers: O) 1957, B) 1960, G) 1963, N) 1965, J) 1972, P) 1973, D) 1974, F) 1975, L) 1980, K) 1984, I) 1989, E) 1990, H) 1991, C) 1992, A) 1994, M) 1995

# Angie's boy child

BY: KATHRYN MORRISH

**It's Christmas Eve and the miracle of birth is happening all over the world...**

I wasn't supposed to be looking in that window. I was supposed to be helping Bert and the lads break into the Post Office but the bus had been late and I didn't make the rendezvous in time.

"They won't half have it in for me not turning up," I muttered to myself as I took a short cut through the woods. And that's when I happened across the cottage. I scrambled up a bank in the dark to find that I was a few feet away from a window. The curtains were open and I could see the flicker of a log fire. A small lamp radiated a soft glow from behind a large settee.

## A small lamp radiated a soft glow from behind a large settee.

"Looks cosy," I thought enviously. I was about to turn away from the window when I heard a cry. I peered into the half-lit room. My eyesight isn't so good nowadays – too many years of close work in various prisons has strained the old peepers. I could just about make out a shape on the settee. A young woman lay there. Looking closer, I saw she was heavily pregnant. There was nobody else to be seen and she appeared to be in pain.

I scanned the room with an old lag's eye – nothing much of value there. Best move on as my tool bag was beginning to make my shoulder ache and I didn't want the damp night air causing a flare-up of my rheumatism. It was Christmas Eve and Madge would be wondering where I was. I'd told her I was meeting the lads for a pint at the Fox and Hounds. She'd only have worried if I'd said about the Post Office job.

I heard another cry of pain and peered into the window again. The young woman's head turned and her terrified gaze met mine. "Help me! Call an ambulance. Please!" she cried.

I'd just 'acquired' one of those new-fangled mobile phones, so what was I to do? I couldn't refuse to phone for help.

"All right, luv?" I mouthed as I tapped on the window-pane. I went to the front door. It was locked. Lucky I had my tools with me. A swift turn of a skeleton key and I was in.

The woman on the settee looked pale, clammy and very frightened. Her dark brown hair lay matted against her forehead.

"The baby's coming early," she gasped. "I'm not due for another month."

"Oh, heck," I said. What did I know about babies? I was a guest of Her Majesty when our two were born, much to Madge's disgust. Never held the twins until they were toddlers.

I tapped in 999. "Emergency services. Which service do you require?"

"Uh, this woman 'ere is having a baby…" I stammered.

"Okay, caller. What is your postcode?"

The woman called out her postcode and the voice said: "The paramedics will be with you shortly. I can talk you through the birthing process, if necessary."

"They'd better blooming well turn up soon," I told her. "I don't know nuffink about babies."

Keeping one ear out for a knock on the door, I followed instructions.

"What's yer name, luv?" I asked as I propped her up into a sitting position and tried to keep her calm. "Angie," she replied through gritted teeth.

"What do they do in films?" I thought. "Lots of hot water and towels."

I made a move to leave the room when Angie suddenly cried out: "It's coming!"

Then everything happened at once. The doorbell rang and I was never in my life so glad to see men in uniform. I let them in and escaped to the kitchen.

As I put the kettle on, a wave of emotion flooded over me, sadness that I hadn't witnessed the birth of my own sons. I should have been there for Madge. What a thing for her to go through without her husband by her side!

PIC: KATE DAVIES

# I couldn't wait to get back to tell her how much I loved her.

What a worry it must have been for her, never knowing if I was going to be inside or at home. My heart filled with gratitude for my loyal wife. I couldn't wait to get back to tell her how much I loved her.

In the meantime, I kept up a supply of hot water and found clean towels in the airing cupboard. As the clock struck midnight, Angie's boy was born. I must admit there was a tear in my eye. Going soft in my old age.

Angie turned to me and asked, "What's your name?"

But I wasn't giving any personal details away. It doesn't pay to stick around too long when you've

done a job. I made my excuses and left.

As I scrambled back down the slope, I realised that it was Christmas morning and I wanted to be with my family.

"Think I'll hang up that old tool bag from now on," I told myself, glancing back at the cottage where I had witnessed the miracle of birth. A miracle that was taking place at this very moment all over the world!

How humbling it had felt to be there, hearing the infant's first lusty yell. I couldn't wait to get home and tell Madge all about it.

"Old habits die hard but I'll stick to my word about the tool bag," I vowed, looking up at the clear night sky and twinkling stars, "or else my name isn't Nicholas Saint."

# December 2010

Wednesday

1

Thursday

2

Friday

3

Saturday

4

Sunday

5

Monday

6

Tuesday

7

Wednesday

8

Thursday

9

Friday

10

Saturday

11

Sunday

12

Monday

13

Tuesday

14

Wednesday

15

Thursday

16

Friday

17

Saturday

18

Sunday

19

Monday

20

Tuesday

21

Shortest Day

Wednesday

22

| | |
|---|---|
| Thursday<br>**23** | Tuesday<br>**28**<br><div align="right">Bank Holiday</div> |
| Friday<br>**24** | Wednesday<br>**29** |
| Saturday<br>**25**<br><div align="right">Christmas Day</div> | Thursday<br>**30** |
| Sunday<br>**26**<br><div align="right">Boxing day</div> | Friday<br>**31**<br><div align="right">New Year's Eve/ Hogmanay</div> |
| Monday<br>**27**<br><div align="right">Bank Holiday</div> | |

## Poetry corner

Don't cry for me when I am gone,
You know yourself that life goes on.
Think only of the time we had,
The things I did that made you glad.

Think of the parties, the dancing too,
The fun, the jokes, the songs we knew.
The children giving us so much pleasure,
The photographs of me you'll treasure.

You'll do, and say, the things I said,
Because they are still inside your head.
We do not die, I shall always be there,
Walking beside you everywhere.

Lift up your head, don't break your heart,
For you and I will never part.
I'll always love you, you know that's true,
So laugh and be happy, I'll take care of you.
**Laura Steer, West Midlands**

## Together forever

PIC: REX FEATURES

# December 6 - 12

## A day to remember

I celebrated my ninetieth birthday in the week before Christmas 2008 and among my presents was a gift token for a trip on the Orient Express. My daughter had arranged it all and was going to accompany me. She made the necessary phone calls and we arranged to go at the end of April, when not only would there be a longer daylight period, but the scenery would be more attractive.

After a pleasant rest in the Orient Express Lounge at Victoria we boarded the train. Incidentally, the carriage we travelled in was one used by the Queen, Prince Phillip and the Queen Mother on occasions! Before long Champagne and canapés were served, followed by a delicious three-course lunch. This was followed by coffee and

Billie about to enjoy her birthday lunch on the Orient Express.

chocolate, which arrived in a beautiful blue and gold box.

We were taken down to Folkestone where a fleet of coaches took us to the second part of our day. We had elected to go to Chartwell, where we had a guided tour of the House and later explored the gardens. We finished up with a cream tea in the restaurant before we boarded the coach for a return to Victoria station. It was a truly wonderful experience and one never to be forgotten.

**Billie Filler, Sunbury on Thames**

## Plant profile

### Gardenia jasminoides

**Height: 3m**
**Spread: 3m**
**Conditions: Plant in moist acidic compost on a bright windowsill, away from sunlight, draughts and dry air.**
This evergreen shrub can only be grown as a houseplant in this country, and usually appears in garden centres during the festive period. Its ivory–coloured flowers shine out against the glossy leaves, producing a truly wonderful scent. Although widely available, it can be a challenge to look after so should only be given to expert gardeners. For example it's a good idea to use tepid rainwater as tap water may be too alkaline.

## Health tip

### Festive phone list

Write down the contact details and festive season opening times of your health care providers here:

**GP out-of-hours number:** .............................................

**Local pharmacy:** ..........................................................

**NHS walk-in centre:** ....................................................

**Dentist:** ........................................................................

## Senior moment

I was at the checkout in the supermarket and with lots of people waiting behind me I couldn't find my purse. After a few moments frantically searching in my bag, the assistant said in a very calm voice: "Excuse me love, is that it under your arm?"

**Joan Garrett, Wilts**

# Fast fact

The origins of your humble toothbrush date back as far as 3500 BC, when the Babylonians would use frayed twigs to clean their teeth. The Chinese chewing stick followed and then in around 1780 William Addis made the first modern brush in England using swine bristles.

# Small talk

We were in a café and my grandson, Charlie, asked for a drink. "What is the magic word Charlie?" I asked. As quick as a flash he said: "Abracadabra!"

**Mrs Story, London**

# Fashion we wore

**T**his photo was taken in 1951, showing my friends and me in the Girl's Life Brigade. We're all showing off our stripes – I'm second from the right – the sergeant! We belonged to the 1st Tottenham Company, which was a large brigade, taking girls from 5 years old upwards. We had many happy times and went to a lovely big house in Bexhill for our summer camp (very cushy!) which is where this photo was taken. I still keep in touch with some of the girls from that time. Our time there gave us a great grounding in self-control, discipline and morals.

**Margaret Morley (née Skitter), Enfield**

# Recipe of the week

## Thai chicken, pumpkin and broccoli curry
### Serves 4

◆ 1 tbsp sunflower or vegetable oil
◆ 1 onion, chopped
◆ 3 cm (1¼ in) piece of ginger, peeled and finely chopped
◆ 2 cloves of garlic, finely chopped or crushed
◆ 75 g (3 oz) red curry paste
◆ 2 chicken breasts, cut into bite-size pieces
◆ 1 medium pumpkin or butternut squash, peeled and cut into 2 cm (¾ in) pieces
◆ 1 tbsp fish sauce
◆ 400 g (16 oz) can of coconut milk
◆ 200 g (8 oz) Tenderstem® broccoli
◆ 150 g (6 oz) baby corn, halved
◆ 1 x bunch of spring onions, sliced
◆ Juice of 1 lime
◆ Bunch of coriander, roughly chopped
◆ 300 g (12 oz) Thai rice, to serve

1. In a large wok or frying pan, heat the oil and gently stir-fry the onion, ginger and garlic for about 5 minutes, or until softened but not coloured. Add the curry paste and chicken, and cook for a further minute.
2. Then add the pumpkin or squash, the fish sauce, coconut milk and 200 ml (8 fl oz) water. Bring to a simmer and cook uncovered for 15 minutes.
3. Add the broccoli, baby corn and spring onions cook for a further 5 minutes, or until the vegetables are tender.
4. Finally, stir in the lime-juice and coriander and serve immediately on top of piles of boiled Thai rice.

Recipe: Tenderstem® broccoli, www.tenderstem.co.uk

# A love for quilting

For years I've done sewing of all sorts, making dresses for my daughter – I even managed to make a shirt for my husband. Work and bringing up my family limited my available time for sewing until I retired. With time on my hands between gardening and decorating I wanted to do something new. A friend showed me her patchwork quilt and I was hooked. I took the opportunity to pick her brains (and borrow a multitude of her quilting magazines). I came home laden with books and ideas for quilts.

My next job was to collect all my bits of material that I had hoarded over the years into what is called your 'stash'. I had a lot of fabric that I couldn't remember buying, all safely put in a big plastic box

Quilting is Trish's favourite new hobby.

ready for my first quilt. A visit to a quilting website gave me a wonderful display of fabric to choose from. Of course, for a quilt you need wadding, but what thickness? I didn't know that I'd have such choice. A quick phone call to my friend sorted that problem. With renewed confidence I ordered an array of cloth and wadding. I'm now in my element with fat quarters and log cabin – just a couple of terms used in the new world I've found in quilting. So far I've made two quilts with another one in progress. And I can't wait to start my next one – I have so many ideas.

**Trish Wapling, Uxbridge**

## Plant profile

### Mahonia media 'Charity'

**Height: 3m**
**Spread: 3m**
**Conditions: Thrives in well-drained, moist soils and prefers a shady position.**

An architectural masterpiece, with spiky leaves and stalks of scented yellow flowers in winter, this shrub deserves a place in every garden. It looks great in a woodland setting and should be placed so its winter blooms can be enjoyed by those fair-weather gardeners who remain inside until spring returns. Widely available from garden centres.

## Health tip
### Snack maths

Before you indulge in too many mince pies remember that the average pie has 360 calories – to burn off those calories a woman weighing 11st 7lbs would have to walk 6km. Ask yourself – is it worth it?

## Senior moment

I phoned my sister and got no answer, I kept trying but I couldn't get a reply. Later my sister phoned back to say that when her phone rang she had been saying 'hello' to her remote control. No wonder I couldn't get through!

**Mrs Robinson, Leicester**

## Fast fact

Coronation Street was first aired at 7pm on December 9, 1960. Ken Barlow is the only remaining character who appeared in that very first episode. He's been married four times, widowed twice and divorced once. And he's had an impressive 27 girlfriends!

## Small talk

My partner Don has a habit of putting the word 'my' in front of anything he watches regularly on the TV. We had been minding the grandchildren for the day, and when I took them home, I left Don watching 'his' football. When the eldest, Ellie, got home she saw her Dad was watching the football, too. "You can't watch that," she said, "It's granddad's!"  **Paula Howarth, Lancs**

## Fashion we wore

**T**his picture was taken in the Fifties when we were on holiday in Yorkshire. My dress was a blue and white corded cotton and, as someone remarked, always looked 'bandbox' fresh. At the time I was working in a shop in Rippon called Philip Hall. I bought this dress from there, along with a yellow one with black spots – both of them made me feel really special. The car, a Morris Minor, was borrowed for the holiday. In later years I had a Morris Minor myself, which was always a pleasure to drive and really reliable.  **Mary Pickard, Stafford**

## Recipe of the week

### Christmas meringue snowmen

**Makes: 5 snowmen**

◆ 2 large Lion Quality egg whites
◆ 100 g (4 oz) caster sugar
◆ 75 g (3 oz) milk chocolate drops
◆ 5 x 10 cm (4 in) lengths of tartan ribbon
◆ Icing sugar, for dusting

1. Preheat the oven to 140°C/275°F/Gas Mark 1. Grease a large baking sheet and line with baking parchment.
2. In a large clean bowl, whisk the egg whites until they form stiff peaks. Add a third of the sugar and whisk until the mixture is stiff and shiny. Repeat with the other two-thirds of sugar.
3. Using a dessert spoon, place 5 rounded heaps of meringue, about 6 cm (2½ in) in diameter well spaced on the baking sheets. To make the heads use a teaspoon to place 5 rounded heaps, about 4 cm (1½ in) in diameter well spaced again.
4. Bake for 1 hour, or until the base of the meringues feel dry and crisp. Leave to cool.
5. To decorate, reserve 10 chocolate drops for eyes and melt the remainder. Using a small paintbrush, paint a blob on top of each body and place a head on top.
6. Then wrap the ribbon around the neck of the snowman, securing onto the snowman with chocolate.
7. Finally, glue two eyes onto each snowman with chocolate and paint a chocolate smile onto each face. Dust with icing sugar.

Recipe: British Lion Eggs, www.eggrecipes.co.uk

Jacky's dad

# My war

I was about five years old when the war broke out. The first I knew about it was when my father, who was a policeman, was called up. He became a Military Policeman in the Eighth Army and was posted to the Middle East in 1941 – he didn't return home for five years. Mum's three sisters came to live with us at this time as my grandmother had to move to a smaller house and also had four sons to cope with as well.

Life carried on and our neighbours were so friendly, helping us out as much as they could. Times were very difficult, but we still managed a singsong and a laugh at get-togethers with family and friends. The letters from our Dad were a highlight and when Mum replied I was allowed a couple of lines at the bottom of the page, always the same message 'When are you coming home Dad? – love Jacky'.

When the war was over and we knew dad was on his way home we decorated our part of the street with flags and bunting and a big 'Welcome Home' banner. We weren't sure of Dad's exact arrival date, but knew it would be soon.

One Saturday afternoon I was returning home after visiting my grandmother when I met a neighbour on the corner of the street. Looking at me with a smile she said: "Your Dad's come home." I ran the rest of the way home and the house was in uproar. There in the front room in his army uniform was my Dad. That was the end of my war.

**Jacky Udall, Bristol**

## Plant profile

### Chimonanthus praecox

**Height: 3.9m**

**Spread: 3m**

**Conditions: Thrives in well-drained soils and a sunny sheltered position. Plant it against a south-facing wall if possible.**

Position this shrub close to a doorway so you can enjoy the scent on a warm winter day. One sniff of this shrub's intoxicating perfume and you'll realise why its common name is Wintersweet. Its flowers are really pretty, a combination of light sulphur yellow and purple, and are borne on bare branches. Widely available from garden centres.

## Health tip

### Mistletoe kisses

A kiss on the cheek under the mistletoe is fine, but don't shake hands unless you want to catch every bug going. If you can't avoid it wash your hands as soon as possible and avoid touching your nose or mouth.

## Senior moment

Before going out for a meal my friend and I spent half an hour looking for my glasses. In desperation we even looked in the dirty washing basket! Giving up, we went to the restaurant, where I remembered the only place I hadn't looked, in my glasses case!

**Sheila Lague, by email**

## Fast fact

One of the highest-rated soap episodes in British television history was screened on Christmas Day 1986. A whopping 30.15 million viewers tuned in to see Den Watts hand over divorce papers to his wife Angie.

## Small talk

I asked my three-year-old great granddaughter, Emily, what she'd left for Santa. Expecting her to say a mince pie, she calmly replied: "A list!"

**Gwen Harris, Cambridge**

## Fashion we wore

This is a photo of my friend, Doris, taken in 1958, when she was 21. The suit she's wearing was kingfisher blue. It always looked very smart, worn with a crisp white blouse and black court shoes (her black handbag is hidden behind her back in the picture). Doris and I have been friends since primary school. We live a few miles apart and meet up regularly. After more than 65 years we're still never lost for words.

**Sylvia Peers, Flintshire**

## Recipe of the week

### Sophie Conran's chicken and mushroom pie

**Serves 4 generous portions**

- 1 kg (2 lb 1 oz) chicken pieces
- 1 onion, halved
- 1 large carrot, peeled
- 1 stick of celery, sliced
- A few sprigs of parsley
- 25 g (1 oz) butter
- 3 tbsp plain flour
- 250 g (10 oz) baby button mushrooms, halved
- 3 tbsp chopped fresh parsley
- 300 g (12 oz) ready-made puff pastry
- 1 egg, beaten
- Salt and pepper

1. Simmer the first five ingredients with 1 litre (1 ³/₄ pts) water for 1 hour, or until the chicken is tender.
2. Break the chicken into rough chunks, discarding the bones. Reserve the stock but discard the vegetables.
3. Reduce the stock to around 600ml (1 pt)
4. Preheat the oven to 200°C/400°F/Gas Mark 6. In a large saucepan, gently melt the butter, stir in the flour and cook for 1-2 minutes. Pour in the stock and bring to the boil, hand whisking all the time until the sauce thickens.
5. Stir in the mushrooms and simmer for 4 minutes. Season to taste, before adding the chicken.
6. Roll out the pastry and roughly cut round a 1.5 litre (2½ pt) oval pie dish. Use the remaining pastry strips to line the dish edges. Spoon the filling in and brush the pastry rim with water before laying on the pastry top. Pinch to seal and brush with the egg.
7. Make a steam hole in the centre before placing on a baking tray for 25 minutes, or until the pastry is golden brown. Serve with boiled potatoes and carrots.

◆ **Top tip:** The chicken and stock can be prepared the previous day

Recipe: Mushroom Bureau, www.mushroom-uk.com

# A Christmas arrival

**M**y mum was rushed into hospital the week before Christmas 1955. Her baby wasn't due to be born until the end of February, but on December 22 Judith and Jacqueline were born. No one knew Mum was having twins so it was a big surprise. Both the babies were very tiny, Jacky weighed 3lb 4oz and Judith weighed 1lb 7½ oz. We were told not to expect too much and that they probably wouldn't survive. Jacqueline died the next day but Judith was still fighting. I remember going to the hospital to see her in the incubator when she was just a few days old – she looked like a little skinned rabbit. She was bright red and very wrinkled. She wore a ladies' handkerchief as a nappy because they hadn't anything small enough to fit her. She also wore a little doll's bonnet but no other clothes.

Christmas was a bit flat that year. Mum and Dad spent most of the time at the hospital. Judith

Margaret with her baby sister Judy.

eventually came home at Easter weighing around 5lbs. She was still very tiny but at least she looked like a baby now. I loved helping to look after her and feeding her whenever I could. I used to take her for long walks and my friends got a bit fed up seeing me with a baby all the time. I think this is probably why we have stayed so close, because of all the time I spent with her when she was small.

**Margaret Palmer, Peterborough**

## Plant profile

### Rhododendron simsii

**Height: 35-50cm**
**Spread: 30cm**
**Conditions: Plant in moist ericaceous compost and place in a bright cool room, out of direct sunlight.**
Labelled as an azalea in the houseplant section of the garden centre, this half-hardy species usually flowers in spring but is brought on in a greenhouse to flower at Christmas. Think cool, moist and shady and your plant will thrive. A host of colours are available, ranging from white through every shade of pink to purple. Ensure the roots remain wet at all times and feed weekly. Plant outside in spring and bring in before the frosts.

## Health tip
### Be thankful

Take stock of the last year and make a list of things to be thankful for. It's a great way to enhance your wellbeing and boost your mood, as psychologists believe that gratitude could be the key to happiness.

## Senior moment

I recently found a watch that I hadn't worn for years. I fancied wearing it for a change but it wasn't working, so I took it into the jewellers for a new battery. I asked the assistant if I could come and collect it the next day and what the charge would be. "Oh, you can have it now for free," he replied cheerfully. "It's a wind up!" Didn't I feel a fool!

**Marion Beaney, Berkshire**

## Fast fact

The Queen's first Christmas speech was transmitted on BBC radio in 1952. In her speech she gave a special mention to those who were serving their country in distant lands. It wasn't until 1957 that for the first time the Queen delivered her speech live on television from Sandringham.

## Small talk

My granddaughter Niamh was talking about Christmas the other day. We were discussing Father Christmas, when she asked: "How many radiators has Santa got?" It took me a while to realise she meant reindeers!

**G Welburn, by email**

## Fashion we wore

My wife, Elizabeth and I were married in September 1951 and spent our honeymoon in Bournemouth. The photograph shows us walking along the promenade. As usual I'm wearing a collar and tie and jacket – there were no jeans, t-shirts or trainers in those days. We stayed in a hotel, paying £11 2s for both of us for one week. As we were still on ration books I seem to remember the meals provided were pretty awful. But as I was demobbed from the Navy a few years earlier I was no stranger to second-class meals.

**John Dunn, Wrexham**

## Recipe of the week

### White chocolate and cranberry baked apples
Serves 4-6

- 6 medium Bramley apples, peeled, cored and halved
- 50 g (2 oz) butter, melted
- 50 g (2 oz) caster sugar
- 6 tbsp cranberry sauce
- 75 g (3 oz) white chocolate, roughly chopped
- 25 g (1 oz) flaked almonds

1. Preheat the oven to 180°C/350°F/Gas Mark 4. Lightly grease a shallow ovenproof dish and add the apples.
2. Drizzle over the butter and sprinkle with the sugar. Gently toss until the apples are evenly coated. Arrange the apples, cut side up, in a single layer and bake uncovered for 15 minutes, or until browning slightly.
3. Spoon the cranberry sauce over the apples, stirring to coat then scatter over the chocolate and almonds. Bake for a further 10 minutes, or until the apples are fully tender.
4. This can be served hot or warm with dollops of ice cream or clotted cream.

Recipe: Bramley Apples, www.bramleyapples.co.uk

# I remember Crackerjack!

BY: MARION CLARKE

**H**ands up anyone who still owns a Crackerjack pencil! There must be hundreds of them out there as they were handed out as a consolation prize to almost every child who appeared on this long running BBC TV programme. The joke was that they were kept in a special locked cabinet – a cunning ploy to make them appear more valuable than they were. Well, whatever the reason, Crackerjack pencils became a much coveted status symbol – proof that you had actually been on the show.

Crackerjack was launched in September 1955 when it was presented by Eamonn Andrews. The last programme went out on in December 1984 when the front man was Stu Francis (whose famous catchphrase was 'Oooh, I could crush a grape!')

In its early days, music and comedy was provided by Pearl Carr and Teddy Johnson but later on many big names in the pop world – Tom Jones, The Who and Status Quo – made guest appearances

## Crackerjack pencils were much coveted

The programme was filmed in front of an audience of youngsters who all shouted 'Crackerjack' very loudly whenever any of the presenters spoke the magic word. During its run, it was presented by Leslie Crowther, Michael Aspel and Ed Stewart who were, at different times, ably assisted by

Eamonn Andrews with young contestants taking part in 'Double or Drop'.

PIC BBC PHOTO LIBRARY

Pip Hinton, Jillian Comber and Sarah Hollamby.

Assistance was particularly required in the hectic quiz game called Double or Drop. Each contestant was given a prize to hold for every correct answer and a cabbage if they got it wrong. They were out of the game if they dropped any of the items or when they received a third cabbage.

Things got even more manic when a new game, Take a Chance, was introduced. This was the one in which a celebrity guest could score extra points for the contestant they were teamed up with. Failure to answer questions correctly resulted in the celebrity guest or Stu Francis being covered in gunge.

Equally popular was the comedy duo Don and Pete (Don Maclean and Peter Glaze). Peter played the pompous one who was always being told by Don not to get his knickers in a twist. This gave rise to much hilarity as knickers was still quite a naughty word back in those innocent times.

Among other Crackerjack regulars were Basil Brush and The Krankies, a husband and wife comedy team. Jeanette dressed up as a schoolboy called Wee Jimmie Krankie.

It was all good clean fun (except for the gunge) and for generations of children the weekend started with the announcement: "It's Friday, it's five to five – it's Crackerjack!"

# Brain-teaser

# Quiz of the month

All these events took place in the month of December over the past 60 years, but can you arrange them in the order that they happened?

PIC: REX FEATURES

**A** Women who wish to have oral contraception will now be able to get it on the National Health Service.

**B** Thousands of people flock to cinemas in the UK to watch the long-awaited blockbuster, Star Wars.

**C** The Prime Minister, James Callaghan, has challenged MPs to decide if his government should remain in power or face the people in an early general election.

**D** The gates isolating the people of Gibraltar from Spain have been opened to pedestrians after 13 years.

**E** The first heart and lung transplant operation to be performed in Britain was successfully carried out today on Swedish journalist, Lars Ljungberg.

**F** The British and Irish prime ministers have signed The Joint Declaration of Peace which they hope will end 25 years of bombing and murder in Northern Ireland.

**G** Stuntman Eddie Kidd has accomplished a 'death-defying' motorcycle leap – crossing an 80 foot gap over a 50 foot sheer drop above a viaduct on a 400cc motorcycle.

**H** Millions of British and Commonwealth listeners have heard Queen Elizabeth's first Christmas broadcast of her reign.

**I** Hundreds of people have died from the effects of toxic gases which leaked from a chemical factory near the central Indian city of Bhopal.

**J** Health Minister Edwina Currie has provoked outrage by saying most of Britain's egg production is infected with the salmonella bacteria.

**K** Former futures trader Nick Leeson has been jailed for six-and-a-half years for his part in the collapse of Barings Bank.

**L** Former Beatle, John Lennon, has been shot dead by an unknown gunman who opened fire outside the musician's New York apartment.

**M** Donald Campbell has broken the world water speed record – travelling at 273mph in his boat Bluebird.

**N** Deposed Romanian president Nicolae Ceausescu and his wife Elena have been shot by a firing squad after a secret military tribunal found them both guilty of crimes against the state.

**O** Administrators have been called in to try to salvage the Maxwell business empire, which is at least £1bn in debt.

**P** A mysterious epidemic, which has been discovered in homosexual men, is causing increasing concern in the United States.

News stories taken from http://news.bbc.co.uk/onthisday/

ANSWERS: H) 1952, A) 1961, M) 1964, B) 1977, C) 1978, G) 1978, L) 1980, P) 1981, D) 1982, E) 1983, I) 1984, J) 1988, N) 1989, O) 1991, F) 1993, K) 1995